T0301153

OUR COUNTRY IN CRISIS

OUR COUNTRY IN CRISIS

Britain's Housing Emergency and How We Rebuild

KWAJO TWENEBOA

First published in Great Britain in 2024 by Trapeze
an imprint of The Orion Publishing Group Ltd
Carmelite House, 50 Victoria Embankment
London EC4Y 0DZ

An Hachette UK Company

1 3 5 7 9 10 8 6 4 2

ISBN (Hardback) 9781398719262
ISBN (eBook) 9781398719286
ISBN (Audio) 9781398719293

Typeset by Input Data Services Ltd, Bridgwater, Somerset

Printed in Great Britain by Clays Ltd, Elcograf, S.p.A.

MIX
Paper | Supporting
responsible forestry
FSC
www.fsc.org
FSC® C104740

www.orionbooks.co.uk

This book is dedicated to my dad, who I miss terribly, and to my family and mum, who I appreciate greatly.

For the bereaved friends and families of the Grenfell victims, the family of Awaab Ishak and to the many thousands who have suffered or died because of homelessness or disrepair, I also dedicate this to you.

Finally, I dedicate this to my online followers who have empowered my voice.

Contents

'Home is where one starts from.'
                  – T.S. Eliot, 'East Coker'

Foreword by Daniel Hewitt

From the outside, there appears to be nothing unusual about Harris Primary Academy in Peckham Park, South London. On any weekday morning, you will find the welcoming smiles of hi-vis-clad teachers standing at the school gates, mirroring the bustle of beaming faces being dropped off by their parents as they file in for another day of learning. More than 300 children aged between four and eleven are taught there – and over half of those children are homeless. It is a remarkable, repugnant reality that should shame us all.

Behind the smile of each child is a story of instability and despair. They arrive at school having spent the night in a homeless shelter, a hostel, a bed and breakfast, or on the floor of a family friend's living room. They live transient lives in temporary homes, often cramped, squalid flats, forced to share beds with their siblings or their parents. They may have lived this way for days or weeks, sometimes months; for some, it may be all they have ever known. Some of the children leave for school from one hotel, only to be taken to a different hotel when the school day has ended. A chronic shortage of available properties also pushes them out of their local area, many miles from school, meaning a mammoth commute across the capital, sometimes lasting more than an hour, before the day has even begun. Long journeys for small legs.

For the teachers of Harris Primary Academy, this is 'the new normal' – the housing crisis is so dire that it is the children in stable, secure housing that stand out, not those who are homeless.

What hope is there for this nowhere generation of children? What little life they have so far lived is defined by uncertainty. They are victims of a housing crisis that each day casts its net wider, trapping and traumatising families, and setting in train untold damage on young lives with no choice or voice in the matter – damaging their education, their physical and mental health, their prospects, their ambitions, their relationships, their view of power and authority.

Britain is full of these stories of shock and shame, squalor and systemic inequality. A voice is the *least* they deserve – if only there were more people able or willing to listen to them, and to tell their stories.

Journalism, the industry I have worked in for over a decade as a television reporter, has had too little to offer by way of attention and exposure to the real-life impact of Britain's broken housing system. Housing is chronically under-reported as an issue in relation to its size and significance. Newspapers and broadcasters have health and science correspondents; transport and education reporters; sports and media editors – but there are very few dedicated housing reporters.

Politically, housing has simply not been a priority for Britain's biggest parties. The role of Housing Secretary is seen as a stepping stone for ambitious ministers coveting so-called higher offices of state. It has long been a government department junior ministers use to impress the prime minister of the day in the hope of promotion. The UK has had fifteen Housing Ministers since 2010. Unlike Health, Education or Transport, housing was not even viewed as important enough to have its own dedicated departmental title – it was wedged between 'Levelling Up' and 'Communities' and before that, local government, until Lee Rowley was appointed as Minister for Housing on 13 November 2023. It was not just the Conservative Party, though – under New Labour too there was no named Housing Secretary of any kind. It was, in fact, Theresa May as prime minister who reinstated Housing as a Cabinet-level title.

Yet housing affects all of us, in myriad ways. Whether through rent or mortgage payments, housing costs are most people's biggest financial expense, and those costs are growing. Safe, secure, affordable housing is the bedrock of happy, healthy lives. Where we live determines so much else. Home is where we start from.

There is a vital debate to be had as to why housing has been treated so often and for so long as a secondary issue by our political and media classes. It may be partly and perhaps crudely explained by the fact that, on a personal level, it *is* a secondary issue for the majority of those in senior positions in politics and the media – most in senior positions have been fortunate enough to live during a period when the cost of housing, even in London on a modest salary, was eminently affordable. Buying a home or finding a reasonably priced place to rent was not the near-impossible task it has become today. How many of today's MPs or journalists grew up in a council house, or have been unable to afford to pay their rent, or have been forced to live in temporary or substandard accommodation?

That is why Kwajo Tweneboa is such a vital voice in this debate, and the debate about the future of Britain. I first met Kwajo in May 2021 on the Eastfields housing estate he'd been living on in Mitcham, South London, with his late father. Two months earlier, I had begun an investigation into social housing conditions, and had walked into a tower block in Croydon and witnessed the worst housing conditions imaginable. In one flat, where a single mum was living with her two young children, a small, persistent leak she had reported to her landlord, Croydon Council, had been ignored for months and allowed to spread uncontrollably. The walls of her home were covered in thick, black mould; water had soaked the carpets and their clothes and made its way into the light fittings, putting their lives in danger. The flat was not fit for human habitation. Other flats in the block were in the same squalid, dangerous state. The conditions were barely believable and totally unliveable. When we aired our findings on *ITV News*, we received an avalanche of emails and messages from thousands of tenants from across the country experiencing disrepair, and being ignored by their landlords. It was through my investigation that I learned of Kwajo's experience.

Yet Kwajo was not just talking about the horror he had personally endured with his father. He instead wanted to highlight what his whole community had been facing for decades. He would become the voice of his entire estate, and later the voice for others around the country. Social housing tenants saw in him not only someone who cared, someone who understood and lived their experience, but, crucially, someone willing to do something about it. To stand up. To fight. Stories were there to be told, and Kwajo was willing to tell them, and to shame those responsible. In doing so, he has done more to bring attention to the importance of safe, secure housing than anyone living in Britain today – and with it, he has provided a glimmer of hope for those children at Harris Primary Academy, and beyond.

Preface

This book was written in 2023, with the anecdotes, experiences and facts drawn from six years of campaigning and research. All of the dates, facts and figures were accurate at the time of writing, but there will no doubt be shifts and changes in the world by the time this book launches. I welcome that, and hope in the future I could update this book with the progress made.

The housing crisis is a messy and unwieldy entity, and in this book I have simplified certain strands of it to help us get back to the core of the issue, as well as to hopefully make this book more accessible and engaging for the people this crisis impacts most – the working class. Now, I understand that class, especially what constitutes someone to be working class, is difficult to nail down, but in this book I understand working class to mean those who face the realities of low income and no wealth *currently*. There are many who identify as working class who are not, or who perhaps have been and are not any more, but in this book the people I am focusing on are those who are directly experiencing this crisis, facing extreme poverty and are on the waiting list for or are living in social housing. As Vicky Spratt identified in her book *Tenants*, 'In 2015, the British

Social Attitudes (BSA) survey found that 60 per cent of people in Britain identify as middle class.' However, she also revealed that 'the 2021 edition of the BSA survey found that 47 per cent of Britons in what sociologists would consider to be 'middle-class professional and managerial jobs' identify as 'working class'. Social class is subjective and mouldable, and we need to remember that.

I have changed names of those in the book who didn't want to be identified, but all of the stories included in this book are real, and many were witnessed by me first-hand. If I was not there to witness events I have made efforts to interview and speak to those who were. This book is about sparking a conversation, drawing attention to those people who should be amplified within the conversation. I know my book is important because it's one of the first that is by someone who has directly experienced the impact of this crisis, and mine is a voice that usually goes unheard in these conversations. I have done my best not to intellectualise this subject because it is too raw, too real and too current, I believe, to do so. I understand I am not the leading voice or expert in this space, as I have reinforced a number of times. However, if I am to be the entry point, then I hope this book will build an understanding of the core parts of this crisis and will spread awareness. I have included further reading in this book to point to key books where anyone can deepen their knowledge of this crisis, and I hope you will support these authors just as you have supported me.

Introduction: My Story

I was born in King's College Hospital, South London, in 1998 to a working-class family. Both of my parents worked hard in the health and social care sector as carers looking after the elderly and vulnerable – that's how they met. Growing up, we definitely had to make the most of what we had; we didn't have the latest of anything, but our parents always made sure we had clothes on our backs, food, heating and a roof over our heads. As I got older, I could see that they struggled financially more than others did, but one thing I know for sure is that we were given the very best that our parents had. I always thought that secondary school felt like my best years – I went to a state school, and I was never the most intelligent, but I got by. Back then, it felt like the only thing my friends and I worried about was whether we'd get our homework done in time. The first time that veneer started to crack was when I was twelve years old and my family was evicted from our home. It was the first time that we had experienced the cruel and destructive consequences of the housing crisis.

I remember us sitting with our belongings in Merton Council's civic centre, my dad having to speak to several members of staff about how we'd been made homeless, and we needed somewhere to stay. His pleas clearly fell on deaf ears. As a child, having to sit there in the civic centre and declare yourself homeless was one of the most boring and embarrassing things you could do. We had to stay there all day, morning until evening, just to prove that we had nowhere else to go. I wouldn't have had the words to describe it at the time, but looking back, the whole process was really dehumanising. I remember as a child sitting there thinking *I hope nobody from school sees us.* Even though we were asked to sit outside the meetings, we still could hear pretty much everything said in the room. Our dad always had a folder with his paperwork and letters neatly sorted when we went to the council, and it included doctors' notes too. We'd hear him telling them about his medical conditions, including his depression, and there was nothing for us to do as children but sit and listen. I remember so clearly how patronising they were to him. He was often dismissed by staff who always seemed in a rush to get the conversation over and done with, as if they had something more pressing to do. They listened to respond instead of listening to understand.

That winter was bitterly cold as we walked the streets from hostel to hostel after school, not knowing where we'd be night after night. When we did get a hostel for the night, I remember drying our cold, wet socks on the radiators because our feet were freezing, the skin on them all wrinkled as our shoes were soaked through. There was a point where we slept in one of those big yellow storage units, on top of the furniture that was being stored there from our old flat. We had to sneak in and out every night and morning so that we weren't caught, and then go off to school and pretend like everything was normal. My siblings and I never spoke about it, but I know we were all thinking and going through the same things, and it was traumatising and upsetting for us all. My sisters were thirteen and ten at the time and it goes without saying that we didn't discuss anything about being homeless or our situation with anyone at school. As a matter of fact, with anyone at all.

Back then, I knew that we were homeless, but we never quite acknowledged our situation as 'homelessness'. As the years progressed, things were a bit more comfortable – we'd finally been moved into another property, and it felt like everything was going great. Then it all came crashing down when we were evicted from another place we called home because the landlord wanted it back, and the cycle started again because renting privately from anywhere else was cripplingly expensive. I was in my last year of sixth form by this time, and my sister was about to sit her GCSEs – my goodness, it was stressful. When we were evicted, there we were again at the civic centre, and this time Dad was given two options: move to Luton or go into temporary accommodation. The ultimatums they give people don't take into consideration current circumstances at all. Considering we were in school and had lived in London our whole lives, temporary accommodation was the only option – we couldn't just pack our bags and move to Luton. When we agreed though, we had no idea how flexible their definition of 'accommodation' would turn out to be. We ended up being moved into a badly converted garage, with the garage door still on. The bathroom was about the size of a broom cupboard, and damp and black mould seeped from the wardrobe and grew on the bed frames. Just in case we weren't uncomfortable enough, there was an infestation of ants and the place was freezing cold.

I remember waking up one morning and getting ready for sixth form – my dad had the news on, and they were showing the fire at Grenfell Tower live on TV. For me, that's when I truly realised on a wider scale that social housing tenants just weren't cared about. They were neglected, abused even, and were so clearly seen as worth less than everyone else in society. What made it even worse was the demographic of victims and families in the tower; it was the first thing I noticed as I watched. I found out later that 85 per cent of the residents who died the night of the fire were people of colour, a fact that hits me even harder when I consider that it accurately reflects the demographic of tenants who have reached out to me for help when I travel around the UK.

In 2018, after years of bidding, my dad was finally given a Clarion Housing Association property, but the joy of finding somewhere permanent to stay wouldn't last long. The property was in complete disrepair: damp, mould, cockroaches, mice, woodlice, water filling the bathroom light fixture, holes in the walls, a bath that was unfit for use, rotten kitchen units that we found out were nearly a hundred years old, broken back garden fences, a broken back door and even asbestos. Even with all of these problems it felt like a sigh of relief to have a permanent roof over our heads after the pressure my dad had felt battling the council waiting lists for years. We complained to the landlords over and over again about our living conditions, but nothing was done. We were greeted with silence each and every time. It was later that same year that my dad was diagnosed with stage 1 oesophageal cancer. I remember being at university at the start of my second year when he called to tell me. I then had the responsibility of calling my brother to tell him, too. I was devastated when I found out, but I was also naïve. The thought that the cancer was 'only stage 1' had me assuming that we'd found it early enough, and therefore Dad would be treated for it and would get better, but I had a lack of understanding about his cancer and just how aggressive it was. Looking back on Christmas that year, I know that at the time I thought he just wasn't hungry when he barely ate anything. The truth was that I hadn't realised he physically could no longer eat due to the mass in his oesophagus. Not long after, he was hooked up to a machine to receive chemotherapy. That would be one of his last Christmases.

As 2019 progressed, Dad began to get weaker and weaker and less talkative. He went from walking around to not having enough energy to finish a sentence. From eating and drinking to throwing up every five minutes because he was unable to swallow his own saliva. He had been the kind of person to look after others, and now he was the person being looked after by nurses three times a day, the person to be fed through his stomach. They often say having cancer is one of the worst things in the world, but watching someone close to you deteriorate is just as awful, and I can say first-hand that is the case. It's almost like having sleep paralysis – you want to stop it progressing, you want to wake up and find out it's all a dream, you want to change things, but instead you're forced to watch and suffer. I didn't understand how destructive the disease was. No one close to me had ever passed away or had cancer, so watching my dad have it felt like a massive blow I was completely unprepared for. Like being hit by a bus. The conditions of the property were becoming more mentally challenging, too. Knowing Dad was so ill, bed-bound, receiving medical treatment to try and save his life, while around him there was vermin, damp and mould felt completely unfair. Thinking back, that is one of the saddest parts of all this. Living and dying in a home not fit for human habitation. The thought is haunting.

I remember being so stressed at work too as I had two jobs at the time. I was doing an internship at Enterprise Rent-A-Car and during the summer I was working in GAP, too. I was often working six days a week, every other week with twelve-hour shifts, all the while worrying about Dad's declining health. Eventually I decided to quit my job and move to a different one in a school with fewer working hours and weekends off so that I could try to balance home life without feeling overwhelmed. There was one morning a few days before I moved jobs when my sister called me to come to the hospital – she had found Dad having a seizure and he was unresponsive. When I got there, I was told they had found a mass on his brain, and they thought it was the cancer spreading. We later found out it was a cyst from an infection. Dad's feeding tube had fallen out a couple of weeks before my sister found him fitting. He'd been in bed in the property when the tube fell out, and a new one was reinserted where he lay, in completely unsanitary conditions. My family and I had no doubt his home environment had a direct link to the infection which caused the cyst on his brain.

Dad was due to have surgery to remove his tumour, but instead he had to have brain surgery to drain the cyst – with the recovery required from that, his body couldn't take another major surgery. He died on 21 January 2020 at 6.13 a.m. I remember a mixture of emotions: relief that it was over and that he was at peace, depressed, drained and angry at the fact that my dad was lost to me. More than anything, I felt resentment that his last few months were spent in such terrible conditions. How he wasn't seen as a priority or treated in the same way that he had always treated others. I don't think grief has a definitive feeling, it's too large to contain in words.

In the aftermath I was angry and sadder than I had ever been before – I ended up being diagnosed with severe depression and anxiety. I even felt suicidal. I couldn't stop feeling bitter at the level of disrepair we were living in as we tried to navigate through the worst time of our lives. I was too ashamed to bring my friends home at a time when I needed support the most. The day of his funeral, we had a major leak causing the partial collapse of a ceiling. Even though we complained about it in February 2020, nobody came out to look at it until months later, in October. All of the other problems still existed. Eventually they pulled the ceiling down, but they failed to let us know that it contained asbestos, and they left the dust everywhere. I remember asking when the new ceiling would go up, and I was told January of the following year, so we'd be left without a ceiling for months. The house was freezing. By that point I had already contacted a solicitor and opened a legal case, but still the landlord dragged their feet. We were promised repair dates time and time again, but they either got cancelled or nobody showed up. I found myself spending more time at work on the phone trying to chase repairs than doing my actual job – on one of those phone calls they just hung up on me.

I had reached the end of my tether, so I decided to take pictures and videos of the conditions we were forced to live in and upload them to Twitter. I'd had enough at that point; I was exhausted and depressed, and it became very clear that was the only move I could make. Even though at that point I was still ashamed about how we were living, and my friends didn't even know about any of it, I knew that shame could no longer be a part of the equation if I wanted my situation to change. I figured that the worst that could happen is I would be insulted and maybe blamed for the conditions, but it was quite the opposite. My tweets went viral. There was a real outcry when people saw it, the local news picked it up and that is where my story started to change. The landlord finally responded with: 'We're sorry Mr Tweneboa feels as though he hasn't received the service he deserves.' Nothing to me could have been more insulting. That one line was a lightbulb moment for me. I decided it was me versus them, and I knew that this was a battle I was going to win. I visited every single home on my estate, looking inside and collating footage of the conditions people were living in on my phone, uploading every second of it to Twitter. The reaction was instant – again I went viral. This time, a team at ITV News who had been investigating poor living conditions got hold of it. The team consisted of Daniel Hewitt, Sarah O'Connell and Sophie Alexander, whom I now consider good friends, and for two weeks we worked with tenants to film how they were living. It went out on national news and was met with outrage from people across the country, including Members of Parliament. The ball was finally in my hands, and the housing provider was disgraced into carrying out hundreds of repairs on the estate and issuing a public apology after being grilled and publicly shamed by the ITV housing investigations team.

I knew that my work was not over, and this problem was much bigger than my estate, so I went to other local estates that were managed by the same organisation. I discovered that thousands of tenants were living in similar conditions. So I did what I do best: I shamed the landlords and associations who were responsible. It was the beginning of a pattern of work I'd become really familiar with – I started travelling across the country on behalf of tenants to post videos and images of their housing, putting the pressure on landlords to respond. In some cases, tenants were given new homes and moved out in under forty-eight hours after I had posted online. My following grew, and so did the shared sense of outrage and the list of tenants coming forward, showing the scale of the problem.

In the eighteen months that followed, I went from living in disrepair myself, to advising government officials on policy, meeting Grenfell United and Shelter along with other organisations, and going on news programmes to talk about poor living conditions that millions face. Recently, I presented my own documentary, highlighting the state of housing in the UK and the horrific conditions people are living in, including someone's home which was flooded with raw sewage. I feel a great sense of fulfilment from the work I have been able to do, even though I wasn't able to do it while my dad was alive. I am motivated by him; I want this to be his legacy.

In writing this, I want to lay out the facts. I want it to be raw just like my work. I want to be direct, impactful – sometimes shocking and uncomfortable because the truth unfortunately is. My family is proud of the work that I'm doing, and the fact that it's impacting the lives of so many. They've become more actively involved themselves in keeping up with politics and issues affecting those who are worse off, and they're as frustrated as I am at the way that tenants are treated, especially after Grenfell. I know they are with me, and that spurs me on. With this book, my hope is that by sharing my story, the facts, the realities and how I see the future, I can inspire more people to become more actively involved in change like my family and I have become. As a young Black man from a working-class estate, this is what we go through, and the reality isn't rosy. But many voices are hard to ignore, and if we face this together, we could build something better.

Part One:

How We Got Here

It's not hard for it to feel like the end of days living in the United Kingdom at the moment. Each crisis feels more overwhelming than the last and often it's hard to work out where to direct your attention. Politicians want that. When we're angry, afraid, anxious and confused, they know we are looking for someone, anyone, to tell us how to fix our world in simple and concise ways. That's exactly what they did with Brexit. 'Oh, you are struggling right now? Why don't we just leave the European Union?' And of course, none of the rewards have appeared in the way we were promised. They achieved their political goal, and individuals around the country were left to pick up the pieces.

What we need to face up to and understand is that the three pillars of our society – housing, health and education – that so desperately need to be upheld and sustained, are buckling because they have not been repaired or reinforced for far too long. There have been botched paint jobs for sure, but when the foundations are crumbling, what good does that do for the long term?

In health, it's clear for anyone who has tried to book a doctor's appointment recently or is trying to get the time and attention of a medical professional in the NHS that times are bad, and resources are low. In fact, the number of hospital beds in England have halved over the past thirty years, yet populations are continuing to increase.[1] Chronic understaffing, poor retention, insufficient funding, deteriorating estates and long waits are just some of the key issues the NHS is facing right now.[2]

In the education system, similar funding and budget cuts are having a real impact along with teacher retention, Covid catch-up and pupil mental health.[3] The education system has arguably not been fit for purpose for many years, with the curriculum measuring all children's abilities against the same archaic idea of what is exceptional and what isn't. It's like judging a fish on its ability to climb a tree. Fish are great swimmers, but you're not seeing that. On top of this, children are coming to school hungry, and the cost of living is so serious that many have to rely on the school for their only meal of the day.

Then there's housing, which is one of my main sources of frustration. I've experienced first-hand the neglect that is being allowed to happen and the disrepair that is costing lives. I've seen horrific things that many of you reading will not believe, and I'll be outlining some of these later in this book. This isn't just social housing, this is about private tenants, too. We all deserve somewhere safe and secure to live, but in recent years many people haven't been able to afford to live anywhere, and for those who do have some-where to stay, they often have to cope with conditions that impact hugely on their quality of life.

These issues are expansive and far-reaching. It isn't just the most impoverished people in our society who are facing the brunt of this, it's almost everyone aside from the elite few. And yet, it is often the elite few making decisions about our lives and our futures. Something has to give, and the voices of the masses need to be heard. For those of you who have seen me on TV or social media, you will know that I'm not afraid to speak up, to put my head above the parapet and call people to account, regardless of my age, background or the colour of my skin – and from what I've experienced it's clearly needed. The progress I have been able to make in the housing sector has been largely because I've been loud, honest and unrelenting. And this is a message I want to carry through in this book. It can feel really hopeless at times, believe me I've been there. It can seem like nothing will change and that all you can expect from life is the shit hand you've been dealt. But that doesn't have to be; we can turn it around. We can join our voices together in a resounding and unanimous shout, telling those who have the power that they must step the hell up and make change happen.

Reinvesting into society is exactly what is required for our country to no longer be in crisis. Short-term sacrifices might be needed, granted, but if we take care, fund our welfare systems and reinvigorate the basic pillars that support us, we can turn things around and the benefits will be felt by everyone. We've done it before, we can do it again, and that's where I want to start.

A Very Short History of the Welfare State, Social Housing and the Right to Buy

It was after the Second World War that the incoming Labour government introduced the welfare state. It was a revolutionary move applying recommendations from pioneering civil servant Sir William Beveridge. The aim: to wipe out poverty and hardship in society.

The wars had taken a toll on Great Britain, just as they had on the rest of the world. Pre-war there had been an economic depression, and during the war, people faced severe austerity, trying to make a life during a time that was characterised by instability and chaos. Today, we can hardly begin to imagine it. Lives were intensely difficult, often punctuated by loss and devastation. When the war ended, the British were hungry for change and so they voted in a Labour government that promised to do so. The Beveridge Report of 1942 offered a brave new vision for the future that spelled out a system of social insurance covering every citizen, regardless of income. And so it was – Labour secured 393 seats in the House of Commons, and what followed were six momentous years of social change.

I believe we are reaching this point again. Following the impact of Covid, the exposed lies and turbulence of the Tory government and the growing unrest of the nation, there is the possibility and potential that we could see this renewed trust in a Labour government that will reaffirm the social insurance that Beveridge originally proposed. Well, I'd hope so at least. From 1945 to 1951, while Labour was governing, the social reforms began in earnest. The 1944 Education Act introduced compulsory free secondary education for all. In 1948 there was the birth of the National Health Service. A massive programme to build social housing commenced, and in the 1950s, councils were building on average 147,000 homes a year. It soon went mainstream and in the 1960s a quarter of all the country's housing was council housing.[1] All of these things vastly improved the lives of UK citizens. It wasn't a utopia by any means, and it didn't see the end of all problems such as unemployment, wealth disparity and debt. There is an argument that winning the war meant solutions weren't as extreme as they needed to be because we still had our economic class structures and systems intact, unlike Germany, for example. Of course, social and economic equalities were still evident. However, the Labour government in these years made more significant changes than any other government before and since.[2]

Progress had been made, whether the Conservative governments liked it or not, and for the most part they had to admit that the improved welfare of citizens was helpful in other ways. Of course, it was largely selfish in that they

were happy that the lower classes were being more productive and making them more money because they were
happier, better looked after, had fewer health issues, better
education and somewhere safe to rest their head at night. It
wasn't going to take long before someone would take steps
to undo all of the good social work that had been done, and
reinforce the hierarchical structures that serve the powerful.
And this is where we come to the moment that, to me, is
the obvious catalyst that led us to where we are today. It
can be traced back through consecutive governments who
failed to act, all the way to Margaret Thatcher and the Right
to Buy scheme.

It was 1980, and only a year into Margaret Thatcher's first
government, that a Housing Act was created 'to give . . . the
right to buy their homes . . . to tenants of local authorities'.
It was a fuelling of consumerism and individualism, and it
was enticing; the terms were generous, and so the wheels
of Right to Buy were set in motion. Imagine how it must
have felt for working-class individuals on estates when the
government sold them that nice shiny idea? 'Oh, you've
always wanted to buy your home? Now you can! We can
give you the opportunity to do so.' People were quick to
buy their homes, but Thatcher and her Cabinet failed to
mention to anyone that as the available social housing was
sold off and as the income started to feed its way back into
government and local authorities, that they had no plan to
replace any of the housing.

This incentive, which on the surface sounded positive,
meant that nearly 2 million homes have been bought since
its introduction in 1980. In 2016, David Cameron promised

7

the reintroduction of the right to buy for housing association tenants up and down the country, meaning the selling off of more public sector homes. Many people ask whether this scheme was a success or not. Of course, there are happy stories that exist because of the scheme – people with limited means or immigrants to the country able to own property and gain security they could never have imagined. But the broader picture is not so positive. In my eyes, the Right to Buy scheme is a massive reason why we find ourselves in this dire situation when it comes to social housing in the UK today.

For example, you are only able to sell your right to buy property after five years, however, you can start privately renting it out straight away. The incentive then is to let out these properties in the private sector in order to generate a profit, but due to the lack of regulation in the private sector, rental prices keep rising, reaching unaffordable heights. In 2013, it was reported that a third of all right to buy homes were owned by private landlords. It was also stated that multimillionaire tycoon Charles Gow, son of Margaret Thatcher's Housing Minister, Ian Gow, owned at least forty ex-council homes on a single council estate. This chills me to the bone. It was also revealed at the time that in Wandsworth alone there were ninety-five landlords who owned and rented out five or more ex-council properties. People who perhaps would have used social housing now have to rent these properties privately that were once social housing for those in need. It is a vicious cycle of consumerism, and so many people are now at risk of being exploited by slum landlords who carve up their properties room by room, forcing upwards of eight people to share one bathroom and one kitchen. The largest leasehold landlord owned the leases of ninety-three of its freehold properties. These are the realities we have to face.

The idea of selling off council homes was something that existed even before Thatcher's Right to Buy scheme – during the 1920s, council homes were sold 'on a small scale'. During the 1950s, sales accelerated: 5,825 in May 1956 alone. By 1972, even a distinctly leftist Tory environment secretary, Peter Walker, could declare to his party conference that the ability of council tenants to buy their homes was a 'very basic right', and that they should be offered a 20 per cent discount on the market price.[3] Even the Labour governments in the 1970s began leaning towards the idea of home ownership being a priority. As such, Labour governments, when in power, built progressively fewer council homes. Still today, the home-ownership agenda continues to be pushed by politicians. You would hope that at least one politician would look back over the last forty years and think, *maybe this isn't working?* In 1977, a high-profile housing study by the Callaghan administration accepted that 'for most people, owning one's house is a basic and natural desire.' While I can appreciate that it may be a 'natural desire' for most, it's also true that most people would simply desire a roof over their head that they can afford, a space of their own that won't cave in on them or make them sick. Over the years, language used by Labour and the Conservatives to talk about the housing issue was beginning to converge.[4] Social housing, once seen as a safety net for a large section of society, would soon become starved of necessary priority or investment and feed what we now see as a housing crisis, many decades on. In 1979, there were 6.5 million council homes; in 2022, there were 2.2 million.

Since this point, multiple prime ministers have made pledges to build more social housing and then failed to follow through. From 1980 to 2021, 1.8 million households bought a house from their local authority through the scheme. Last year, approximately 5,500 social homes were built, in spite of the 1.25 million people on the waiting list for social housing. There's a lot of information that's been hidden behind the 'affordable housing' statistics, but social housing only forms a very small portion of those inflated statistics that mayors and governments praise. At this rate, it will take 175 years to build enough housing just to clear the current backlog of requests, and yet no one has prioritised housing in their budgets for years. To rebuild would now cost billions; because the issue has been left for so long, solving it almost becomes unfathomable. The cost of temporary accommodation, managing the crisis this has created and the pressures on all of our public services that have come as a result, has probably cost the same, if not more than it would have taken to build those replacement homes. The money to resolve this crisis exists, but it seems that politicians have had other priorities for where to spend it, such as on the £100 billion (and perhaps more) currently being funded into HS2, the new zero-carbon high-speed railway.

It comes back to the Conservative agenda, which started it all off and was still being parroted recently by Boris Johnson. Thatcher was pushing their ideals of owning your own home, getting into work. The idea of getting off your backside and working hard to take care of yourself. In selling off social housing, she was encouraging these standards, but by not replacing what was sold and serving those who needed looking after the most, she started the ball rolling towards a society where achieving that original agenda is now, and will be for decades to come, impossible for a lot of people. Could she have known Right to Buy would backfire in this way? Probably not. But then, would she have cared? Given the extreme classism in politics, I think the answer is again, probably not. This classism and attitude towards social housing is not just the fault of the Conservatives, either. We've had Labour governments and mayors since all this began. A big problem is that very few politicians know how to relate to the experience of the working class. Westminster pushes their tick-box exercises around diversity, but how can they be truly diverse if they are not representative of the country they serve? There is hardly anyone in Westminster who can relate to vulnerable people on estates, people living in broken, unfit homes, experiencing these huge pressures. As much as they might try to behave like they are 'relatable', they just aren't. Simply put, they just don't care, or at least don't care about the right and most pressing issues.

I know that politicians would disagree. They would say that 'of course they care', and that they are 'doing everything they can'. But what did they expect us to think when they voted against a bill that would have forced rented homes to be made fit for human habitation? In 2017, 309 Conservative MPs voted against making sure that renters were protected. There are more codes and protections in the

Animal Welfare Act from 2006 than there are laws giving everyone a basic standard of living. For the last twelve years it's been proven that it's just not Conservative by nature to deal with an issue like this, because the assumption is that people's struggles are about laziness. Just look at politicians constantly pushing to 'get everyone back to work'. If a piece of policy doesn't generate financial returns, they just don't focus on it. These issues are going to continue to be costly, both financially and on a personal level, for many individuals because solving the problem won't generate immediate financial benefit. They sacrifice morals chasing cash returns. It's as clear as day – anyone with common sense can see that it is a lack of care, so I don't see why politicians in Westminster can't. This attitude flows through into the conversation around benefits, and the stigma attached to claiming them. It shouldn't need explaining, but not everyone is on benefits because they've chosen to be. A lot of people are unwell – with mental health conditions, disabilities. The idea that they just can't be arsed and don't want to work – this is something you hear again and again. Suella Braverman said only recently that we need to get people off benefits and into work. I'd love to ask her when she last actually spoke to someone on benefits. I guarantee you it wasn't recently, if it ever happened at all. The irony is that the need for benefits is caused by policy.

In 2016, Brandon Lewis, former Minister for Housing and Planning stated that the government would implement deregulatory measures to support housing associations in their objectives to help move tenants towards home ownership and deliver an additional supply of new homes.

Boosting the number of sales to tenants would generate an increase in receipts for housing associations, enabling them to reinvest in the delivery of new homes. Housing associations would be able to use sales proceeds to deliver that new extra supply and have the flexibility to replace homes with tenures such as shared ownership. This commitment that more homes would be built, as well as the promise of 'an extra home built for every home sold' fell flat on its face almost immediately. Between 2017 and 2018, there were 20,891 sales of social housing homes. Of the total sales, 12,059 were by Local Authorities and 8,832 by Private Registered Providers (PRP) Housing Associations. Local Authority Right to Buy sales amounted to 11,833, and there were 4,223 Right to Buy sales by (PRP) Housing Associations. That year alone, only 6,463 new social homes were built. A net loss of 14,428 social homes in that short space of time, with an ever-growing social housing waiting list.[5]

This was reiterated in an interview with Tom Murtha. Having worked in several different positions in social housing and spanning many decades, he has an extensive and unique understanding of social housing and was asked about the introduction of Right to Buy in 1980 for council homes and in 2016 under David Cameron for housing association properties. (In 2015, it was even suggested in the *Guardian* that then Prime Minister David Cameron was on track to 'kill off' social housing, and the requirement to build affordable homes.) He said the following:

Tenants who take up the right to buy will receive a discount of up to £104,000 on the sale price, which will be funded from the forced sale of empty council homes. But the offer from housing associations also includes a pledge that all of their homes would be put up for ownership and possible sale in due course. Tenants would be able to buy shares in their own home, for example, and vacant properties could be sold off.

The overall effect of these measures is that the net stock of social rented homes would decline, especially so in high-value areas such as inner London, Oxford and Cambridge. A form of social cleansing of poor people from these areas would take place.

Home ownership rates will no doubt increase, but doing this by shifting homes from one tenure to another without addressing our failure to build enough homes overall is like rearranging the deckchairs on a sinking ship.[6]

That proved to be true, as the government failed to meet building targets and replace the homes that were to be sold off under Right to Buy. Interestingly, in 2016, Boris Johnson, then Mayor of London (and later Prime Minister), criticised the move by the Conservative government, describing it as 'the height of insanity' if it did not lead to the creation of more affordable homes in the capital.[7] I hate to say it, but he was right.

The Right to Buy scheme exacerbated levels of deprivation on estates because some of the homes were now privately owned, and others were not. This meant less funding or coordinated efforts to repair communal spaces, and the communities built up over decades fell apart as many people bought homes and moved out and tenants moved in. My estate in South London is visibly run down from the outside and even worse within its 446 homes. I'd estimate around sixty of these homes have been bought since the 1960s, meaning that around 86 per cent remain social housing. Of those, all that is left are poor-quality social homes in major disrepair. I spoke to my friend Dannika Stewart who lives on a nicer estate in Manchester, and through her own description, it is the polar opposite of the Eastfields Estate. She explained to me that, 'Wealthy people, including celebrities have moved in' and that 'the whole estate has basically been sold off and none of the social homes have been replaced. People were buying their council houses here for a really good deal, especially for the area we are located. Seventy per cent of this estate was council housing when I was a child; now I'd estimate it's around 20 per cent.'

As estates fall into disrepair, they become increasingly undesirable places to live and are at risk of being torn down. An example of this is Robin Hood Gardens in Poplar, completed in 1972. Its innovative, brutalist design has split public opinion, but it was designed to offer safe and stand-out social housing for London communities. According to the V&A, 'it is distinctive for its noise-reducing features, like exterior concrete fins, and for its elevated walkways, known as "streets in the sky", intended to foster interaction between neighbours.'[8] The building has become derelict over the years, with a lack of investment or repair; but instead of seeing this as an opportunity for renovation and restoration, the building is being demolished. The plan is to replace the 252 flats with over 1,500 new homes. Which is a good thing, right? It's very unlikely to be, as it's still entirely unclear whether these new homes will include a higher or lower proportion of 'affordable' housing, and it is unlikely they will include new social homes.[9]

Since its inception, the Right to Buy scheme has become a 'strategic failure', the words used in a damning assessment by the Chartered Institute of Housing.[10] It has decimated communities and exacerbated so many inequalities, many of which I see on a day-to-day basis while campaigning. It has opened the door to social disadvantage on a vast scale. Unfortunately for us, this very short history will take a long time to unpick.

Social Stigma

The working classes have long been stigmatised in British culture. In the years preceding the Industrial Revolution, the difference between the upper classes and lower classes was far more distinct and clear, and the wealth gap more transparent. In the years since, many working-class people may have made positive advancements in terms of stability, however, the reality is that their position has not changed as much as might be perceived and in many cases, it has worsened. There is a reason we are not seeing the disparity so clearly. The mega-wealthy cannot be targeted if they are seen to be not so different to us. In the digital age, we are fed the idea that most of us have access to the lives of the prosperous simply because we can see them. But this just isn't the truth, and you can see the reality of things as plain as day in the data. Equality Trust reports that in 2022, incomes for the poorest 14 million people fell by 7.5 per cent, while incomes for the richest fifth saw a 7.8 per cent increase.[1] And it isn't just in income that we are seeing this. Wealth in Great Britain is even more unequally divided than income. In 2020, the Office for National Statistics (ONS) calculated that the richest 10 per cent of households hold 43 per cent of all wealth. The poorest 50 per cent, by contrast, own just 9 per cent.[2] One pretty jaw-dropping statistic is that by 2023, the richest fifty families in the UK held more wealth than half of the UK population, comprising 33.5 million people.[3]

The demonisation of the working class only fuels a narrative that is preferential to those who have the majority of the UK's income and wealth. They at once want us to feel not so different from them as they want us to feel that the lower classes and the impoverished are vile, dangerous and an untrustworthy minority. This demonisation of the working class has fuelled a stigma that disallows us from treating people who are experiencing hardships for the individual, nuanced and deserving human beings that they are. You may be thinking, *but this isn't about the hard-working ones; it's about the lazy ones who rely on benefits and contribute nothing!* I find it funny that this is the perspective of many working-class people, especially those who no longer live on estates, or perhaps those who never did. The reality is that many of those living in social housing are the hardest working people you will ever meet. For example, Janet, who lives on my estate, is sixty years old, works three jobs, and could teach those in Westminster a thing or two about what it really means to work hard. They wouldn't last a day doing the work she does. This ignorant narrative suggests that everyone is on an equal playing field and that if you simply put your mind to it, you can get yourself out of a bad position. But this has never been true, and just because some people may be lazy and exploiting a system, does that mean the system shouldn't be there for those who are trying

18

and truly need it? If it was so easy to exploit this system, do you think Janet would be working three jobs?

Again, it's important to look at the facts to destigmatise here. The welfare state is a big part of family life in the UK. The *Guardian* reports that 20.3 million families receive some kind of benefit (64 per cent of all families), about 8.7 million of them pensioners. There aren't many families within this that aren't working or trying to work in some form. In fact, the same report found that under 1 per cent of workless households might have two generations who have never worked – about 15,000 households in the UK. It is important to remember that the majority of families experiencing long-term worklessness remained committed to the value of work and preferred to be in jobs rather than on benefits. In-depth research has shown that there was no evidence of 'a culture of worklessness' – values, attitudes and behaviours discouraging employment and encouraging welfare dependence – being passed down the generations. Instead, the long-term worklessness of responsible adults in families was a result of complex problems (particularly related to ill health) associated with living in long-term and deep poverty.[4]

Around 27 per cent of people believe that benefits are claimed fraudulently. This is hard to prove and hard to generalise. The *Guardian* also states that 'in 2012, 18 per cent of working-age households were workless; in only 2 per cent had no one ever worked.' And a big proportion of this number are aged under twenty-five, and so this is likely to be a result of high and rising young adult unemployment. So the broad assumptions aren't hitting the mark. On top of this, there are realities we need to understand when trying to tackle the stigma, for example, 'richer countries spend much more (as a proportion of income) on welfare than poor ones – compare Sweden and Somalia'. Those places without welfare are increasingly unpleasant places to live when there is no safety net to protect those who are the most vulnerable. And the UK isn't spending more than other countries on benefits, in fact we're spending 12 per cent less than France and 19 per cent less than Germany per head. All of the above can be true, and yet stigma persists.[5]

Stigma is still a massive problem within social housing especially, and this is something I have had to battle over the last few years. From the idea that you should feel lucky and grateful to live in social housing to the suggestion that everyone in social housing is living off and exploiting state benefits. The ignorant misconceptions and stigmas are rampant and couldn't be further from the truth. While speaking with Antonio and Ed from Grenfell United, we touched upon the subject of stigma, which is something they both know all too well. It was quite upsetting hearing them speak about this as I could directly relate to what they were saying; my own experience and the experience of many tenants I have worked with over the last few years reflected what they were saying. There is a human impact of stigma where you are constantly told in various ways that you are inferior.

Often with this stigma comes blame. The default is to blame tenants for the conditions they are living in or the situations they find themselves in when it comes to their home. My eyes were really opened to this once I started visiting other tenants up and down the country, helping highlight their cases and witnessing the response to them.

Tenants were often scared to speak out or to be identified alongside the horrific conditions they found themselves in as they automatically expected to be blamed for them. Most of the blame comes from people that live outside social housing as well as those that work for housing providers. With little understanding of building work or the cause of the disrepair, tenants are told that the damp and mould in their property is 'due to their lifestyle' rather than fundamental issues with the insulation or damp-proofing. This has been happening for years. I have seen archived footage from the 1960s and 1970s of tenants being blamed for issues like mould growth. 'Stop drying your clothes indoors,' 'Leave your windows open,' 'You're not ventilating the property,' 'Stop leaving your shower running,' tenants are told. It is never the providers' fault, always those forced to live in sub-par conditions. Many of these homes were not built practically for those living inside them and often cheap and cost-efficient materials have been used in order to knock up the homes. Most recently, we have seen this impacting UK schools that have been built using a certain type of concrete, a cost-cutting material used between the 1950s and 1990s which has now been found to be unsafe and now 'liable to collapse'. How can you expect longevity and quality from something that is poorly constructed, built in a rush and with materials that are of bad quality? I have been into blocks of flats that are only a few years old, absolutely riddled with black mould, flooded from burst corroded pipes, or with sewage running down the walls. These aren't lifestyle issues, this is terrible workmanship and the result of taking shortcuts no matter the long-term cost.

The media also hasn't helped with fuelling the ignorance surrounding social housing and the distaste for those who are more in need of support from the welfare state. Shows created like *Benefits Street* and *Little Britain* only helped to perpetuate a derogatory and offensive depiction of working-class people. *Benefits Street* was a documentary series created in 2014 that followed the lives of ordinary individuals on the breadline. *Little Britain* was a comedy show that portrayed working-class people as stupid, aggressive, disgusting, fat, ugly and disrespectful. Poverty used as a tool for drama or comedy to entertain a demographic of people who believe themselves to be 'better than' should never have been acceptable. The frustrating reality is that those watching these shows were much closer to experiencing the lives of the working-class people depicted than they had ever been to a millionaire or billionaire watching and laughing along with them. Shows like these simply would not exist nowadays due to the insensitivity and for the fact that the cost of living crisis has meant poverty feels like a much closer reality for those of all classes – aside from the most wealthy, of course. However, these shows had done enough damage during their time on screen, with even politicians like former Home Secretary Suella Braverman using the phrase 'benefit street' as an inflammatory attack on those needing support from the state government.[6]

Social housing is often concentrated in specific neighbourhoods or areas with higher levels of deprivation. It's something I noticed more outside London in places like Leeds, Liverpool, Birmingham and Manchester. This clustering of socio-economically disadvantaged communities creates and reinforces negative perceptions and stereotypes, further deepening the stigma associated with being a social housing tenant. In British society, housing is often seen as a symbol of social status and success. When you rely on housing from the state, it is viewed as an indicator of poverty or a lack of personal achievement, irrespective of circumstances. It is sad considering social housing was once looked at as something to be proud of.

Through my work, I have tried to shed light on those behind the front doors of social housing homes. Yes, there are vulnerable individuals who aren't able to work and depend on state benefits. However, there are also many who are hard-working and employed, and I believe unemployed or employed people deserve support. I have met people from a wide variety of backgrounds – local councillors, to supermarket workers, doctors and nurses to solicitors and teachers, journalists to television professionals – all who wouldn't necessarily fit under the depiction and stereotypical idea of a social housing tenant. If you find it hard to believe any of these people rely on welfare, then it shows how pervasive the stigma is. It clouds our thinking so much that we aren't able to see each citizen as a unique, varied individual, with hopes, dreams and desires.

Stigma within social housing can have detrimental effects on the mental health and well-being of tenants. The experience of being stigmatised can lead to feelings of shame, low self-esteem and social isolation, negatively impacting individuals' overall quality of life. Interestingly, I noticed this with myself and the many tenants I've highlighted living in disrepair through social media. The first thing they say is the shame they feel and the worry that they'd be blamed for circumstances and the conditions that they are forced to live in. This makes me sad as really the shame should be felt by a government and system that allows this level of disrepair to continue.

The Problem with Westminster

There is no shame felt in the gilded halls of the House of Commons in Westminster. This is a place of surety, wealth and a confidence that no matter what change officials do or do not enact, they will receive their pay packet at the end of the day – that for most members of the Cabinet is over £100,000, paid for by the lovely taxpayers who can only hope for better days ahead.

The House of Commons, as the primary legislative body in the United Kingdom, plays a crucial role in shaping policies and making decisions that impact the nation. However, the extent to which it represents the diverse socio-economic backgrounds of the population remains a subject of scrutiny. I've been vocally critical of class inequality within Westminster. I've been into Westminster several times, often wearing my tracksuit. I remember the first few times walking in there and being looked at weirdly by security, no doubt because of my clothing as well as the colour of my skin. I clearly wasn't one of their 'usuals'. I looked around Portcullis House and thought two things: one, how extraordinary and grand the architecture was, and two, how out of place I felt. Not a single person resembled me, and I don't mean in terms of clothing. This isn't to say some of these people might have shared my experiences, they may have, but there was no visual display of difference, which is why I stood out like a sore thumb. It was certainly not representative of any estate I'd been in. Everyone seemed as if they were trying really hard to covertly impress one another, as well as simply fit in. It was quite amusing to stand back and watch.

Though I felt out of place, and I often do in the spaces I enter, I am determined not to change myself or carve off parts of myself to fit in with other people's expectations of me. Why should I have to dress as they do, speak as they do, or look as they do in order to be heard? This is the fundamental problem: only a certain kind of person is welcomed into Westminster, despite the fact this is the place where decisions are made that impact everyone. Where were the people that looked like me or the many people I know? It has occasionally made me laugh when I've visited a government building dressed how I feel comfortable and I've walked past 'important people', knowing that if circumstances were different and we passed each other on the street, they'd have a preconceived and likely negative idea of who I am. No doubt they wouldn't even give me the time of day. Yet there I was, in my size-ten Air Max 97s, telling them about themselves in their own front room and feeling pretty great about that.

According to a study by the Sutton Trust in 2020, Members of Parliament (MPs) in the House of Commons are disproportionately likely to have attended private schools. The research also revealed that 29 per cent of MPs elected in the 2019 general election were privately educated, compared to only 7 per cent of the general population. This overrepresentation of privately educated individuals suggests a lack of diversity in educational backgrounds and potentially perpetuates class divides. I would argue there is more class diversity in a loaf of bread than there is in the House of Commons and beyond. I wouldn't be surprised if there was now more class diversity at Oxford or Cambridge than in Westminster. How can you possibly be a truly representative government when there isn't full class representation within the institution?

Diversity has very much become a tick-box exercise, not just in Westminster but in British society. We look at characteristics like race, gender and sexuality to name a few, but there has never been a direct and intersectional focus or exploration of class diversity and its importance. Why is that? Surely, in order to create real change, you need a view from those who are most vulnerable and those who have their ear to the ground in working-class communities? I don't think there has ever been an understanding of this from previous governments, whether they be Labour or Conservative. In fact, I think they'd rather avoid it. To open the doors to those from lower socio-economic backgrounds would open up conversations they simply don't want to have. They don't have to fund higher living wages, build more social housing, improve the education system or reinvest in healthcare if no one is there vocalising why these things matter. For the current MPs, they don't feel the impact of long NHS waiting times when they have private healthcare and they definitely don't see the declining educational standards when they and their parents attended Oxbridge and Eton. There needs to be a huge shift to encourage those from working-class backgrounds to join and engage in politics because looking at the state of Westminster right now it is easy to believe that their experiences are not valid, not enough and not worth any real attention.

Another aspect missing class diversity is the professional backgrounds of MPs. The same study by the Sutton Trust found that 36 per cent of MPs elected in 2019 had previously worked in law, business or the finance sector, compared to approximately 9 per cent of the working-age population. This indicates a higher concentration of individuals from professional and business backgrounds, potentially limiting representation of other professions and working-class experiences. An analysis conducted by the LSE British Politics and Policy Blog in 2020 revealed that approximately 31 per cent of MPs elected in 2019 had a family connection to politics, either through a parent or a close relative. This statistic highlights the influence of inherited political legacies which can contribute to the perpetuation of certain socio-economic classes in political representation.

I think had there been more working-class individuals within Westminster in the previous decades, policies would be of better quality, there would be more discussions on the social impact of policies, and in turn, I believe many more people around the country would be reaping the rewards that come from enacting informed policies. Instead, we have had people from affluent positions making decisions that impact those they have never been able to relate to, and working-class people they simply do not care about.

Party Politics

Before becoming a housing campaigner, I had a very narrow view of politics and the parties that sit on either side of the House, and it was very much influenced by public opinion and media narratives. When deciding to immerse myself in the world of campaigning, I knew that in order to be successful, I needed to be politically neutral – the subject of a broken housing system was beyond party politics or my own personal opinion. Frankly, at that time I couldn't give a shit about politics or politicians. What I cared about was the fact that I was walking into homes that couldn't be classified as such. Homes like Amber's, whose belongings had been destroyed by mould, and Jerome's, whose toilet backsurged and flooded his home with faeces, or Simone's, whose ceiling had caved in more than a year before. For all of them, nothing was being done and for all of them, politics wasn't helping them. And so my focus was, and will always be, on the individuals struggling, as well as the Member of Parliament or party who is interested in fixing this crisis. The situation is now a humanitarian one. I was always up for calling out those I believed were shying away from the issue or blatantly weren't doing what they had promised to do, in order to be elected again. This has been true for politicians on both sides of the House of Commons. And it isn't like they aren't aware of what's going on. I've had to call out MPs for being useless several times, and we've been battling with housing secretaries that are quite frankly, shit, for many, many years. Most of them use the position as a political stepping stone rather than a job that can actively change people's lives. In 2022, I spoke to an MP who told me that, regarding housing, they had received between 5,000 and 7,000 complaints on disrepair alone in the space of a year. That's just in one constituency. There are 650 MPs in Parliament.

The party politics that plays out in government is undoubtedly detrimental to and distracting from addressing social issues in the UK. When political parties prioritise their own interests and ideologies over the greater good, collaboration and cooperation loses and change is hard to come by. This system damages any potential progress in addressing social issues as political opponents often prefer to engage in adversarial debates, resulting in a gridlock and inability to reach consensus or implement effective policies. We have seen that happen with many issues debated off the back of the cost of living crisis.

Parties often prioritise short-term gains, such as electoral victories or satisfying their voter base, over long-term solutions, i.e. investing in the housing sector and reaping the long-term benefits of it. This leads to policy decisions that prioritise immediate political benefits rather than sustainable and comprehensive solutions to social issues. Short-term thinking undermines the ability to tackle systemic problems and provide long-lasting positive impacts on society. It is something that frustrates me as parties are always talking about future prosperity and productivity, yet they often fail to address the issues that so obviously obstruct those goals from being reached. A perfect example of this is Rishi Sunak's recent claims on the net zero transition, and the climate targets the UK are trying to reach. In the lead-up to the election, he has announced a weakening of net zero policies for reasons including: the ban on the sale of new petrol and diesel cars will be delayed, landlords will not be required to upgrade energy efficiency of their homes and meat, dairy and flying taxes will be disregarded. The climate crisis is undoubtedly a pressing issue that should surely not be impacted by the whims of party politics in the lead-up to election time. Announcing this U-turn is a disregard of the social impact on citizens in the hope of a short-term winning of seats. On top of this being a politicisation of a global reality that shouldn't be politicised, most of these claims he's making are untrue (there have never been plans for taxes on flying, meat or dairy).[1]

Changes in government leadership due to party politics can result in policy reversals and instability, too. New governments may prioritise dismantling or reversing the policies of their predecessors, creating discontinuity and impeding progress on social issues. This inconsistency hampers long-term planning, investment and implementation of effective strategies, which often takes many years. The issue with governments playing party politics ends up, in a lot of instances, resulting in prolonged debates and decision-making processes. Political parties may see scoring political points or positioning themselves favourably more of a priority rather than taking swift and direct action to address social issues, as exemplified above. Delays in decision-making can further exacerbate existing problems, prolong suffering and hinder the implementation of necessary reforms.

When party politics take precedence, evidence-based approaches may take a back seat. Decisions may be influenced by political ideologies, public opinion or party interests rather than by rigorous research and expert advice. This neglect of evidence-based approaches can undermine the effectiveness of policies and impede progress in addressing social issues affecting so many.

When there are real lives on the line, we need to cut through all of these whims, debates and silly arguments, and highlight the unrest and crises that are building beyond the stuffy rooms of the House of Commons and Number Ten.

Mismanagement and Deregulation

So you can now appreciate that the situation in government is chaotic at best, neglectful at worst, and this plays out in a number of different ways in the day-to-day. Deregulation is a symptom of this and plays a significant role in destroying what was once a thriving sector. Former Prime Minister David Cameron's bonfire of the quangos (an organisation to which a government has devolved power, but which is still partly controlled and/or financed by government bodies) and introduction of austerity to the UK has led to significant reduction of resource and investment in the public sector. Hand in hand with this was his obsession with the idea of deregulation across most public sectors. He promised to cut red tape in order to make it easier for developers and the building industry, prioritising fast and easy profit-making. This meant that professionals in these industries could get away with cutting corners and evading health and safety expectations. It meant that materials no longer needed to be regulated, and big players had a lot more freedom. With lack of regulation comes chaos, and that's exactly what happened. You fail to regulate, and it becomes a free-for-all.

This was something a prime minister and government should have expected, but it comes back to the point that their priorities have always been elsewhere, and for them, their own political narratives and goals were more important. We must remember that only seven years after the coalition first came into power and decided to bulldoze through regulation, seventy-two people lost their lives in Grenfell Tower. This was a building covered in flammable cladding, one that people had raised concerns about prior to the fire happening. It appears that quality and safety were sacrificed to create quicker, short-term solutions, and this has had a real and lasting impact on lives and, in the case of Grenfell, has ended lives too. We now see across the UK the poor state of some of our buildings and homes, homes built after the coalition government, full of disrepair, and I think it's fair to say this is a direct result of industry-wide deregulation.

For a long time, we had a social housing regulator that failed to regulate. This was one of the biggest shocks I came across while taking on my own housing provider, Clarion Housing Association. When ITV visited my estate and worked with me and other residents/members of the residents' association, I decided it would only be right to report my landlord to the regulator due to the breaches of health and safety. It wasn't just me, either; there were horrific cases of disrepair in most of the properties on the Eastfields estate in Merton. The process of reporting Clarion to the regulator was quite easy. I simply wrote out everything we had found with a list of addresses and conditions relating to each address. I also explained that I too was living in disrepair and told of my concern for the residents as we had been ignored time and again. Once that email was sent I was told I would have to wait a period of time so that a so-called investigation could be carried out and a decision made. I expected members of the regulator to visit the estate to look at conditions themselves, or at least phone some of the residents, including me, for context. None of that happened. I wasn't even contacted to be informed of what the outcome had been. Instead, I came across it in an *Inside Housing* news article weeks later: 'No systematic failure found'.

I was absolutely baffled as to how they could have possibly come to that decision. The estate was falling to bits and the majority of tenants were living in visibly slum-like conditions. Elderly residents were having to visit hardware stores to buy cement, then mixing it in their kitchen to fill holes in walls where mice were coming in. Tenants were advised to sleep in the bath so that the repairs team could come out to fix damage in the rest of the property. A child who had three brain tumours and was in the middle of chemotherapy had to put her hand down the cistern of the toilet in order to pull the chain every time she needed to relieve herself, because Clarion hadn't sent anyone from repairs to fix the toilet. On what planet could 'no systemic failure' have been found?

It was clear to all that the decision didn't reflect reality. My local MP knew this also, which is why they organised a meeting with the regulator to find out how they had possibly come to this decision. It was in that meeting that I would learn one of the biggest lessons about mismanagement, deregulation and how we have reached the point of crisis we are in today. The regulator informed us that after the report was submitted, they hadn't phoned any tenants or visited the estate because it wasn't in their remit and they didn't have the powers to do so. They said what they look at is internal failures within providers at top levels, rather than dealing with direct concerns from tenants. It was hard to wrap my head around. What was the point of a regulator if they couldn't actually investigate and deep-dive into all concerns? There was nothing they could do, they said, and so they pointed us in the direction of the Housing Ombudsman (a person or organisation who investigates, reports on and helps settle complaints). It wasn't the last time I attempted to report Clarion to the regulator for investigation. After visiting other Clarion-run estates in my local area, I found similar if not worse conditions than Eastfields estate. Some blocks showed clear breaches of fire safety, such as lights with water pouring through them and fire doors sticking or having gaps. It wasn't the last time they did everything they possibly could – which felt incredibly close to sweet eff all.

You would hope that the Housing Ombudsman would boldly step in at this point to protect those who needed help and who were going unheard. They deal with complaints about registered providers of social housing in England, including local authorities, about their landlord functions. The Housing Ombudsman is independent and impartial. However, this has been questioned in the past as they are essentially funded by the same organisations they are there to investigate . . . a conflict of interest, some would say. It is a requirement that to be a social housing landlord in the

UK, you must be signed up to this service. I'll be honest, for a very long time, I was unaware that the service even existed. It was a member of the residents' association on my estate who made me aware it was available. After my experiences with the housing regulator, I wondered how useful it would be. Would it be on the side of the tenant? Would the process be drawn out? I had already been living in disrepair for a long time, but would they make the process longer than it needed to be, hoping at some stage I would give up and go away? It is a hidden service that unless you knew they existed, or were vigorously searching, you would likely have never heard of them and you definitely wouldn't know about the support they are there to give.

While looking into the possibility of using them myself, I discovered from other tenants how hard it had been to even get in contact with them, never mind having their complaints and disrepair investigated. Firstly, you need to have a designated representative – either your MP or a professional, which isn't the easiest thing to source. Then there would be an eight-week wait for you to receive a response from the ombudsman service. Now, for someone with sewage flooding their home or whose ceiling has collapsed, this is something they simply don't have time to wait for, and in many of these cases they are in an emergency. Then when it came to compensating tenants for living in disrepair, a lot of the time the amount was so low it didn't even cover the damage of belongings for tenants and in many cases, it was seen as an insulting amount for what they had been subjected to by their landlord. The service is deeply flawed, and needs to be adjusted significantly to be fit for purpose.

This has made taking legal action against a poorly performing provider more attractive. In a legal case the service you are going to receive is very clear. You have a professional surveyor attend your property to carry out a report. You are promised that all necessary repairs would have to be carried out to a satisfactory level and you would also be provided a fair amount of compensation for not only damage caused but also the distress caused throughout the disrepair case. This in itself would be more of an attractive offer for anyone. You understand what you will get and you don't have to jump through multiple hoops in order to get justice. But not everyone has the money to fund legal action, and some cases simply won't be taken on by 'no win no fee' lawyers. During my time speaking with tenants who had suffered or were suffering with active disrepair, they felt the power and influence were on the side of the landlord and the regulators that are supposed to protect them aren't there to serve them at all. In some cases, tenants were having to wait several months, if not a year, for a response from the ombudsman service. This level of poor management of serious cases is catastrophic for families.

Things can change. This is a message I want to reinforce. Though mismanagement and deregulation have been pervasive and are some of the key reasons we've landed where we are, with pressure and activism, we can make things better. I, along with other campaigners and journalists, raised our concerns about the process for tenants to raise their concerns and serious complaints and, as a result, changes were made to the ombudsman service, including scrapping the need for a designated representative. The Ombudsman also took a naming-and-shaming approach to dealing with bad landlords, and in the extreme cases began issuing cases of severe maladministration when terrible service failures had been found. They also increased staff numbers to tackle ever-growing cases of tenants' complaints while rolling out a joint campaign with the government to make tenants aware of their existence and the service they provided, as well as the much-needed changes that they had adopted.

Now, when I speak of mismanagement, I don't only mean the social housing sector. Mismanagement of the private rental sector in the UK has had a detrimental impact on social housing. There is nothing affordable about private renting in England currently, and things are even worse in London with renters paying on average over 50 per cent of their monthly salary on renting.[1] Over the years, a series of factors, including rising rents, inadequate regulation and limited affordability, have contributed to an imbalance that has eroded the availability and quality of social housing as well as increased homelessness. This has all led to an exacerbation of social inequality and a deepening housing crisis. One of the key ways in which the mismanagement of the private rental sector has affected social housing is through the dwindling supply of affordable homes. As rental prices in the private sector have soared, many individuals and families with low incomes have been priced out of the market. With limited alternatives, they have increasingly turned to social housing as a lifeline. However, the insufficient investment in social housing construction and maintenance, coupled with the high demand, has created a shortage of available homes.

As a result, vulnerable individuals and families are left in precarious situations, unable to secure suitable housing.

Margaret Thatcher believed very much in allowing the market to dictate rental prices. What was clear though was that population size was growing and the supply of social housing falling. It could have been foreseen that, as decades would pass, more and more people would depend on private rented accommodation and this, along with other external factors, would mean the average cost of rent would increase. Demand massively outweighs supply, meaning as a result, landlords were free to take advantage of this in the private sector and increase rents. The number of households privately renting has more than doubled over the past two decades, according to the 2021 Census, to 5 million. Average rents across the UK were up 10.8 per cent annually in December 2022. The average Greater London rental property was priced at more than £2,000 in December for the second month on record. Even when you remove London from the equation, rents were still up by 9.4 per cent.[2]

The cost of living has risen faster than incomes in recent years, making it increasingly difficult for tenants to afford private rental properties. As rental costs soar, the gap between housing affordability and income levels widens, placing a significant burden on tenants. This situation has particularly affected low-income households, young professionals and families struggling to secure affordable and stable accommodation. What hasn't helped is the cost of living crisis affecting everything and everyone across the UK. On top of that, the fuel crisis and increased interest rates have meant that the prices of goods and services have increased dramatically. People are having to choose between necessities: food or shelter, shelter or warmth. Landlords have also argued that the increase in mortgage costs means they must increase rents, but the only ones left struggling when that happens are renters. With that being said, there are landlords who see this as an opportunity to make extra income by hiking rents.

Make no mistake, these landlords are fuelling the cycle of poverty and homelessness. Many private landlords have prioritised profit over providing safe and habitable living conditions. This has resulted in substandard housing, with issues such as damp, mould, leaks and inadequate heating becoming all too common. There is little pressure for these landlords to fix issues for their tenants; mostly they will make their excuses and let the problems amass. These poor living conditions can have severe consequences on the physical and mental well-being of tenants. There is a lack of enforcement of regulations on these slum landlords and this allows them to exploit vulnerable tenants with little consequence.

But so many don't have any other option because buying a home is entirely inaccessible, especially around the major cities in the UK. The private rental sector dominates the landscape, and as private landlords focus on maximising profits, their prices become more and more far-fetched and they end up forcing people to look to social housing, of which there is a limited supply. The lack of investment in social housing has perpetuated a vicious cycle, and ultimately granted private landlords with more power than they should hold. They know how they are positioned to continue to exploit tenants and they won't stop unless there is more regulation or consequences. Sky News described the state of the private sector in the UK as at 'breaking point'. Tax hikes for landlords have stopped some from entering the market to make profits, though this has resulted in a restriction of tenants' choice due to low levels of stock available. There needs to be a more significant adjustment to really resolve the problems here.

On top of this, the mismanagement of the private rental sector has contributed to the erosion of communities. The unstable nature of renting in the private sector, with short-term leases and frequent turnover, can disrupt the social fabric of neighbourhoods. It becomes difficult for individuals and families to establish a sense of belonging and stability when they are constantly uprooted due to rising rents or eviction notices. This instability affects the social cohesion and support networks that are crucial for the well-being of communities. This idea of community building was at the heart of social housing in its formulation – and it really worked. There were real benefits and many felt secure, stable and supported in their community setting. Now, that feels like a rarity.

To address the damage caused by the mismanagement of the private rental sector, extensive reforms are needed. This includes stricter regulations and enforcement to ensure that all rental properties meet adequate standards of safety and habitability. Additionally, measures such as rent controls and caps can help alleviate the burden of rising rental costs on low-income households. Increased investment in social housing, both in terms of construction and maintenance, is essential to provide affordable and secure homes for those in need. Furthermore, a holistic approach is required, focusing on the integration of social housing with communities to foster stability and social cohesion. This can be achieved through the implementation of mixed-tenure developments, where social and private housing are integrated to create diverse and inclusive neighbourhoods.

It is clear that the mismanagement of the private rental sector in the UK has had a profound impact on the social housing sector. The dwindling supply of affordable homes, poor living conditions and the neglect of social housing have resulted in a deepening housing crisis and exacerbated social inequality. The situation is so dire that many are choosing not to have children because of the housing crisis. Addressing these issues requires an overhaul of regulation and sector reform, but this can only be executed with increased investment in social housing, coupled with robust regulations and enforcement. Only through such measures can we begin to rectify the damage caused and ensure that everyone has access to safe, affordable and secure housing.

Probably the quickest way there could be positive change is through rent control. Rent control refers to government regulations or policies that limit the amount landlords can charge for rental properties. Unlike some countries where rent control measures are in place, such as Germany, Spain, the Netherlands and even Scotland, England does not have comprehensive rent control legislation. Without rent control, landlords have the freedom to set rents at market rates, which can result in sudden and unaffordable rent hikes, particularly in high-demand areas. This lack of tenant protection exacerbates the difficulties faced by those on lower incomes as well as the affordability crisis. To put this into perspective, the number of postcodes where average monthly rents cost £1,000 or more has more than quadrupled in a year.[3] Average monthly rents hit £2,500 in London and £1,190 across the rest of the UK.[4]

Introducing rent control legislation can provide tenants with increased security and protection against excessive rent increases. Such measures would help stabilise rental costs, ensuring affordability and reducing the risk of displacement and housing insecurity. Rent control policies need to strike a balance between protecting tenants and providing landlords with incentives to maintain and invest in their properties. Alongside rent control, strengthening tenant rights and protections can contribute to a fairer and more balanced rental market. Policies that address unfair eviction practices improve the quality of rental properties, and ensure proper maintenance and repairs are essential to creating a more tenant-friendly rental sector. This is something the government say they want to do with the introduction of the Renters Reform Bill which has been announced by current Secretary of State for Levelling Up, Housing and Communities, Michael Gove, with the removal of section 21 'no fault' evictions, the introduction of an ombudsman service and requirements for all private landlords to sign up to a register. It is hoped this will strengthen power on the side of tenants but also make it clear what expectations are for landlords. Although this is a much-needed positive step in the right direction, lots of people question whether it is enough.

The current situation is the result of decades of mismanagement and deregulation that favours the few, not the many. The scenarios playing out today only serve to keep the 'haves' separate from the 'have-nots'. For those who have worked hard to gain a position on the property ladder, have climbed up the social ranks and are now fair and considerate landlords, the idea of rent controls might be a frustrating possibility, and I have empathy for that. However, we've been living so long without regulation to make all housing secure, safe and affordable, so dramatic action is needed. I believe it's worth the sacrifice.

First-Time Buyers

We've seen how social housing *and* private renting is in crisis, so where have the priorities of our government been all this time?

Well, that's with home ownership and first-time buyers, of course. The culture of home ownership runs strong in the UK, with many believing they haven't 'made it' until they own a home of their own. The government has always promoted and reinforced this message, which has meant renters are often viewed as second class and those in social housing as even more inferior. Leeds Building Society gave the clearest insight when it comes to home ownership over the years in their press release: 'When the Coronation of Her Majesty Queen Elizabeth II took place on 2 June 1953 the average house cost just £1,692 and the average salary was £333. Now, on the eve of His Majesty King Charles III's Coronation on 6 May, it's a very different picture. Over the past seventy years, average house prices have soared and to crown it all, houses are now at their most unaffordable level for around 150 years.'[1]

We are running out of houses, but the demand to own a home isn't going anywhere. In 2010 and 2016, David Cameron adopted a Margaret Thatcher-style approach to housing and pushed the idea of home ownership while slashing funding for social housing and encouraging buy-to-let properties. Tony Blair also encouraged the idea of buy-to-let properties and was in government during the time house prices began to soar, making it virtually impossible for young people to get on the ladder. Between 1997 and 2007, property prices increased by on average 21 per cent per year and sadly, wages didn't follow, which caused a further divide between the haves and have-nots. What governments have failed to understand or realise is that while it is a nice sentiment to own your home, it is currently completely out of touch with the pockets of people up and down the country to do so. With the next election creeping up, both Rishi Sunak's Conservative government and Keir Starmer's Labour Party are again leading their housing proposals with the idea of home ownership.

There is an agenda to this. Home ownership is a symbol of stability, success and personal achievement. By championing policies that support home ownership, political parties aim to appeal to a broad base of voters (the term 'broad' being used very loosely, especially in today's economic climate) who aspire to own their own homes. Promoting home ownership, they believe, resonates with individuals seeking long-term security and financial independence, particularly in a society where property ownership is highly valued. Political parties often use promises related to home ownership as a key campaign strategy to garner voter support. These promises may include pledges to increase access to affordable mortgages, introduce home-ownership schemes, or provide incentives, such as tax breaks and subsidies. Highlighting these policies during general elections makes parties believe it will help differentiate themselves and attract voters concerned about housing affordability and stability.

The government's focus on home ownership is linked to its perception as a driver of economic growth and stability. A thriving property market is often seen as a sign of a healthy economy, as it stimulates construction, generates employment and contributes to GDP growth. Policies aimed at promoting home ownership can potentially boost consumer confidence, help stimulate spending on home-related goods and services and have a positive impact on the wider economy. We now know, however, that in order to have a thriving property market and sector, you must tackle the crisis with a bottom-up approach, otherwise the growth will stall. You cannot build a house on broken foundations and you cannot build a strong economy on disrepair.

Home ownership has been viewed as a means for wealth creation and long-term asset accumulation. By encouraging individuals to invest in property, the government aims to help citizens build equity and financial security. The belief is that property ownership provides individuals with a tangible asset that can appreciate over time, offering a potential source of wealth and retirement security. This is an area, however, that irritates me, because it further perpetuates a divide between the haves and have-nots, and as well as that, wealth is being generated from a need we all have as human beings. Some are able to capitalise on this while the majority have no access to shelter, furthering the divide of inequality across the country.

By prioritising home ownership, the government tactically taps into these social aspirations and seeks to align with the desires and aspirations of the electorate, yet the reality is, especially from what I have witnessed as a campaigner, that by doing so, they also fail to address the elephant in the room, which is that a large majority simply can't attain home ownership. This, however, is something that I don't think will be admitted by any government anytime soon.

It's estimated that over the next fifteen years, the UK will require 5 million new homes – an average of 340,000 a year. This is greater than the government's 300,000 'target' and has not been achieved since 1971. The average number of homes delivered each year over the last decade has been less than half of this figure.[2] It's as simple as supply and demand. We don't have enough housing supply to offer the demand of an increasing population, therefore prices are rising at an unbelievable rate. To get a handle on this, the banks have increased mortgage interest rates, but so much inaction and so many problems amassing over so much time will require more than just a plaster on the problem. The government simply needs to build more housing. It is fundamental for a safe future for everyone and prevents the continued profit-driven property market from continuing to worsen inequality. It would also hopefully allow those who have worked hard to get on the property ladder, instead of renting privately. Fewer private renters means cheaper rents and means fewer people forced to look to social housing.

I have come to terms with the fact I may never be able to own my own home, and this is true for the majority of those from younger generations. What we do know is the only other alternative is to privately rent or live in social housing, and with the current disrepair and exploitation, neither of these routes feels particularly safe or attractive for our future. Nearly 8.4 million people privately rent or are in social housing, with a further 100,000 in temporary accommodation and 1.3 million waiting to get into social housing. Our housing system is broken and demand massively outweighs current supply. Lessons can't be learned unless you're willing to look through a different lens at an issue, and so far the angle has been promoting home ownership *above all*, instead of investing in social housing. That needs to change.

Chronic Underfunding

The chronic underfunding that has continued for decades is something that is having repercussions in all the key pillars of our society. We are seeing it with the NHS and the lack of beds and underpaid healthcare workers. We are seeing it with education and the lack of free school meals for children most in need. We are seeing it in our roads and community spaces which become more and more dilapidated over time. And of course, we are seeing it in our housing, where problems are left to fester.

When housing stock is transferred to housing associations, local authorities pass over direct control and oversight of the management and maintenance of the properties. This takes away accountability for the condition and quality of the homes. From my experience, housing associations have prioritised their own financial sustainability and operational efficiency above home maintenance, which has led to the neglect of necessary repairs, maintenance and improvements. When work is done, it is quick, slapdash and often doesn't resolve the deep-rooted issue. As a result, the quality has massively deteriorated, leaving residents living in slum-like conditions.

As the economic crisis continues, housing associations will argue that they now face resource constraints and financial limitations as providers. They argue that they may struggle to provide and fund adequate resources to address existing issues, leading to a further decline in the quality of homes over time. Perhaps this is true, but then if it is, our government has a duty of care to step in and ensure this doesn't happen. Insufficient investment in repairs, renovations and infrastructure upgrades clearly have contributed directly to the persistence of poor-quality housing. Some housing associations, especially the larger ones, are known to have huge profits in the hundreds of millions, and they can pay their CEOs six-figure salaries, even when resources are limited. Some would argue that their priorities are the issue. What is clear, though, is how much financial pressure local authorities are under and have been under due to cutbacks by the government. Housing associations, as independent entities, may have different priorities and objectives than local authorities. While their mission, easily viewable on their websites, claims to provide affordable and decent housing, their main focus has seemed to be generating income/surplus.[1]

It is important for me to mention that not all transfers of housing stock to housing associations lead to poor-quality homes. In some cases, local authorities have had worse standards of housing than housing associations and it's often harder to get your issue resolved to the correct standard. Some housing associations successfully manage and maintain the majority of their properties to high standards. I would argue that this is done better under smaller housing associations as opposed to their larger counterparts. Proper funding, robust regulation and effective oversight mechanisms are necessary to ensure that transfers of housing stock do not exacerbate the problem of poor-quality homes and that residents have access to safe and decent housing. Sadly, these are things we simply haven't had enough of for generations.

The funding to build new homes has not been there for a long time, and often when it has been funded, the labour used has been poor-quality and produced shoddy work. However, there is another reason we find ourselves in a housing crisis and that is that we simply do not have enough current qualified labour to build the number of quality homes we need. The lack of drive to incentivise young people to enter the construction sector through education, whether that be in college or an apprenticeship, means we now have a generation gap in construction workers who are experienced and skilled. The same exists under social housing providers too, where we have a limited supply of contractors who all seem to be terrible when it comes to standards of work – for example, repairs, plumbers, electricians, builders, plasterers and roofers. It's not just housing where the shortage of labour has been noticed but across construction full stop. Brexit made this situation even worse, with the tightening of immigration rules since the UK left the European Union. This was a huge blow to the industry as we relied heavily on workers from across the EU. A positive is the government has announced they plan to relax immigration rules for builders and carpenters, making it easier for them to work in the UK.

As many of you will be aware, housing isn't the only social issue disproportionately affecting those worst off in

British society. The health and mental health of our society is being failed with a lack of resources. More than 15 million people – 30 per cent of the UK population – live with one or more long-term conditions, and more than 4 million of these people will also have mental health problems.[2] The Royal College of Psychiatrists said its research found that 43 per cent of adults with mental illness say the long waits for treatment have led to their mental health getting worse. Almost a quarter (23 per cent) have to wait more than twelve weeks to start treatment, with many so desperate they turn to A & E or dial 999.[3] It's impossible to not expect a decline in services when there is so little funding into the systems, and the demand continues to grow with the population. You take away food and water from a human and eventually they will die. You strip a public sector of its funding and resources and it will slowly wither away to nothing.

The crisis with mental health in the UK is something that has been acknowledged by the government in the past. In 2019, the government made commitments to increase funding and they created a long-term plan which pledged to increase mental health spending by at least 2.3 billion per year by 2023–24. MIND charity released a report after conducting a freedom of information request to mental health trusts. The report stated that four in ten mental health trusts (41 per cent) have staffing levels well below established benchmarks. Only a third (33 per cent) of respondents who came into contact with NHS services when in crisis were assessed within four hours. Only half (56 per cent) of crisis teams accept self-referrals from known service users and just one in five (21 per cent) from service users that aren't already known to them.[4]

Mental health can affect absolutely anyone, no matter your background, but what is obvious is those from disadvantaged backgrounds are more likely to struggle with their mental health. Those most vulnerable have the least stability in all areas of their lives, and I have seen those struggling and trying to fight through disrepair on so many fronts. It is soul-destroying. The majority of people that I've spoken to say that the poor conditions that they live in affect their mental state. Many are on antidepressants.

This area of healthcare reflects a much bigger issue across the NHS. Just like housing in the UK, the NHS has probably experienced its worst decade since it was established in 1948. It's fair to say that this hasn't been helped by the unprecedented Covid-19 pandemic, but some would argue that signs the NHS was struggling were showing long before the pandemic. From ambulance delays to long waits in A & E to a lack of staff, years of austerity measures and budget constraints have left the NHS grappling with inadequate resources to meet the growing demand for healthcare services. Despite periodic funding increases, they have often been insufficient to address the mounting pressures faced by the healthcare system. Multi-year funding increases and a series of reforms resulted in major improvements in NHS performance between 2000 and 2010, but performance has declined since 2010 as a result of much lower funding increases, limited funds for capital investment, and neglect of workforce planning.[5]

The National Health Service has long been regarded as a cornerstone of the country's social fabric, providing healthcare services to millions of people. However, by looking at the current state of the NHS, you would never be able to know how highly valued it is in society. Currently, the NHS faces a multitude of challenges that impact its ability to deliver timely and high-quality care to patients. Staffing shortages play a huge part in this. The healthcare workforce, including doctors, nurses and other healthcare professionals, is stretched thin due to increasing patient demands, staff attrition and difficulties in recruitment and retention. NHS England says the health service is already operating with 154,000 fewer full-time staff than it needs, and that number could balloon to 571,000 staff by 2036 on current trends.[6] The strain on healthcare staff contributes to excessive workloads, leading to burnout and impacting the quality of care provided. Moreover, the shortage of personnel affects the NHS's ability to respond effectively to emergencies and hampers efforts to improve patient outcomes. This can be seen in the very real average response time for people requiring an ambulance for a stroke, severe burns or chest pain, which is ninety-three minutes, five times the operation target of eighteen minutes.[7]

The infrastructure of the NHS is also showing signs of strain. Outdated equipment and insufficient investment in infrastructure maintenance have led to a deterioration in the quality of care provided. Patients are often treated in outdated and overcrowded hospitals, leading to compromised patient comfort, increased infection risks and difficulties in maintaining adequate standards of cleanliness. Last year, someone reached out to me on behalf of their relative who was receiving treatment for a stroke in hospital. They were concerned and shocked by the conditions, and rightly so as there were mice droppings across the hospital ward and the room the patient was staying in while receiving treatment. This is not the fault of those hard-working individuals who are fighting to keep the NHS running; it is the result of there simply not being enough resources to keep facilities adequately clean and sterilised. This state of disrepair and the lack of investment in modern healthcare infrastructure hinders the NHS's ability to keep pace with advancing medical technologies and to provide state-of-the-art care to patients. There are real people behind these statistics and facts who are suffering, but there are no signs that the upcoming governments will make a U-turn and show generosity to a healthcare system that used to be the most envied in the world.

The final pillar to a strong and healthy society is education. The education sector, especially state schools, has faced the harsh reality of budget cuts and strict austerity measures since 2010, and this is having an impact on children's learning in scary ways. Having attended and worked in a state school myself, I've seen the impact chronic underfunding has had on the quality of education, as well as on staff members who entered the sector with passion and are unable to achieve the progress they'd hoped for due to forces beyond their control. Since leaving the school that I worked in and after the height of the global pandemic, I've spoken to many teachers and education professionals who all express common concerns, explaining that it's becoming increasingly difficult to do the jobs that they love and that they are looking to leave because the stress caused by over-working and being underpaid is insurmountable.

Teachers are slowly but surely leaving the profession, and now there is a dearth of teachers who are qualified and experienced. Teacher recruitment has become difficult over the last decade and turnover is at an all-time high. Now, ultimately, this is going to impact the students and the quality of their education, the attainment gap, and also their future opportunities. Without the stability of teachers who know them and therefore notice gaps in their knowledge or struggles they may be facing, children are neglected. The importance of consistency for students as they are growing and learning can be the difference that can build them to see real success in the future. I think most people can think of a teacher who had an impact on them. Now imagine that person not existing, and imagine you had little support at home, or that you were neurodivergent or had accessibility needs. Do you think you would have survived, let alone thrived? I know I wouldn't have. It concerns me deeply that students are being set up for failure through no fault of their own, and that this crisis is disproportionately affecting those from poorer backgrounds.

Since 2010, investment in schools has been falling – in real terms, funding fell by 9 per cent in the decade to 2019, and, despite recent efforts, won't return to 2010 levels until next year. Soaring inflation has meant that teachers have had a pay cut of 5 per cent between this year and last, on top of a 13 per cent cut in the last decade.[8] Subjects like physics and maths have been understaffed for so long that there is no room for a further squeeze. Soon some schools will simply not have a physics teacher. Without the funding, the inequality gap will grow. There will be those who can afford to pay for their education and excellent resources, and those who can't. There will be those who go to school full, and eat a meal provided, and those who go to school hungry and don't even have a free school meal, due to cuts. There needs to be a shift. All children, no matter their background, deserve a strong education.

Instead of ongoing, chronic underfunding, we need to see markedly increased funding and investment in the three pillars that are essential to our society. By upskilling our society with great education, keeping people healthy and ensuring they have safe and secure places to live, we are boosting our economy and maximising our input. The long-term gains are undeniable, but it would require politicians to see past the end of their noses, something I've learned they aren't particularly good at doing.

The Cost of Living Crisis

The cost of living crisis is the most recent crisis to enter our vocabulary. The cost of living crisis refers to a period during which the cost of everyday essentials like food and bills increases more quickly than average household income, and this has been the case for the UK since the beginning of 2021.[1] This has had a profound impact on people's lives, affecting their financial stability, well-being and overall quality of life.

Struggling to pay for everyday essentials is nothing new for many in the UK, but this crisis has plunged hundreds of thousands of people into poverty. It's now begun to affect nearly everyone in the UK; those who are from working-class backgrounds to middle-class backgrounds and even the wealthier middle-class backgrounds too, from those working in schools, hospitals and housing to those who work in the media or as civil servants and in jobs that were considered well paid only a few years ago. Of course, this crisis is disproportionately affecting poorer households who were already fighting to keep their power running, their central heating on and putting food on the table. The high inflation driving the cost of living crisis is a global phenomenon, but the degree of exposure to it in the UK has been increased by policy choices.[2] One of those is the government's decision to cut the rate of the main benefit, Universal Credit, in one of the biggest ever overnight cuts to benefit. This drove many into a hardship that is difficult to imagine.

Rising housing costs, rent, fuel prices, utility bills, transportation costs and the general increase in the prices of goods and services have made it increasingly difficult and for some, totally impossible to make ends meet. Throughout the crisis we've seen stories of nurses eating patients' leftovers, parents having to skip meals and some putting themselves into debt to pay for essential resources. Worryingly, almost a fifth of low-income families are in debt to high-cost lenders, including loan sharks, amounting to £3.5 million in debt.[3] This leads to reduced savings, a constant state of financial insecurity and, for many, total bankruptcy.

The housing crisis has played a central role in the cost of living crisis – all of these things are connected and this is why my book could never have just been about housing. Skyrocketing house prices and a lack of affordable housing options have made it increasingly challenging for individuals and families to find and maintain affordable accommodation. This issue was made worse by the mini-budget in 2022, causing interest rates to soar. Many are faced with the burden of high rental costs, limited housing options and the constant fear of being priced out of their communities. Home ownership has become an elusive dream for many, with steep deposit requirements and unaffordable mortgage repayments. Rates have now hopefully peaked after the Bank of England's base rate reached 5.5 per cent in August

2023, but as at December 2023 that rate has remained stable for the past four months and due to the rate of inflation now having reduced significantly, there is hope that reductions in interest rates could be seen in the early part of 2024.[4] This housing instability has far-reaching consequences, affecting individuals' mental well-being, family dynamics and overall morale of the country. The cost of living crisis also has had broader societal and economic implications. As individuals and families are burdened by financial pressures, they have had limited disposable income to spend on non-essential goods and services. This reduced consumer spending has a direct impact on local businesses and the economy as a whole, leading to a slowdown in economic growth and job losses across different industries.

Since the beginning of the cost of living crisis, we've seen an increase in rates of crime across the United Kingdom, and in some cases, people have resorted to illegal activity to simply survive, stealing food to feed their children or defrauding money to pay their bills. In one London borough it was revealed that the most stolen item from supermarkets was baby formula, and in another borough the most stolen item was Calpol. Between 2022 and 2023, it was estimated that there were nearly 8 million incidents of theft in British shops and that's since 2016–17. Incidents of theft have more than doubled in that space of time with people stealing items from bread to milk to toothpaste as well as other basic supermarket items.[5] Supermarkets have resorted to placing security tags on some of these items, for example, milk, washing powder, steaks and deodorant. The fact that these goods aren't luxury goods shows the desperation from those worst off and the lengths that they're having to go to in order to survive. One in twenty-five adults admitted to not scanning some items or incorrectly scanning items at self-checkout in supermarkets for things that they can't afford but need.[6] Crime is wrong, we can all agree on that. However we have to extend some empathy to the people who have been pushed into desperate conditions and can see no other option than to steal.

The use of food banks has also dramatically increased. Once upon a time, food banks were only used by those who were below the poverty line, but what we've seen in the last few years is even those in full-time work have to go to food banks just to make sure they can continue eating every day. It has become so common that food banks are now worried they will run out of food. It angers me that we even need food banks, and this is something that I've said for many, many years. The fact that we have accepted their existence, and that to see a long queue outside a food bank is not an extraordinary sight is sickening. We have seen politicians stop by food banks, taking pictures and posting them on social media, and this absolutely floors me because these are the same people who have the power to reduce the need for this charitable work. We have gone from shame in the existence of them to pride in those who volunteer at them and serve their communities.

In my campaigning work, I've spoken to people that have been alive more than double my lifetime who say they've never experienced an economic situation this bad, and I've spoken to people who say they haven't struggled so significantly in decades. With all of this, can we really be surprised at the high rates of mental health issues or the increase in rates of suicide? People have been pushed to the absolute limit. I have met a lady who was devastated that she was having to borrow money from her older children in order to pay her bills, rent and feed her younger children. She cried to me that the disrepair in her house compounded by her dwindling finances was all becoming too much to bear. I think the worst thing I have noticed in my work is that during the winter, so many families can't even afford to put the heating on, resorting to wearing layers and layers of clothes, even to bed. For families with damp and mould this is even harder because they are routinely told that to tackle that issue they must ventilate the property, but to do that they have to have the windows open and be even colder than they already are. One lady I spoke to was spending £70 every few days to keep her heating on while the windows were open as it had recently snowed outside, and they had no other option but to do that or freeze. There are reports during the winter too that people were resorting to lighting candles in their homes instead of using their lights and electricity because it has simply become unaffordable. And although the government said that they would help discount the increase in gas and electric bills, for many, it doesn't go far enough. Last winter, there were dire reports of the elderly left to freeze in their homes, and many going into libraries and public spaces where it was warm so they didn't have to pay the extortionate prices.

This will sound like normality to many, but an absolute nightmare to others. In all of this, there are those who are profiting. The energy providers for one, but also the politicians as they can use most of these troubles as political fodder to help attain power. There are those who have the power and the ability to help the most vulnerable and turn the state of our country around, but it requires sacrifice and selflessness – something that historically, those with influence are reluctant to do. It's important to understand this, as often the narrative is placed on those most vulnerable to help themselves. To work harder, to save more, to 'buy a new kettle' or to be more frugal. All of these things won't resolve the decades of neglect and active damage the leaders of our country have wrought. But they don't want us to look at them; they'd rather punch downwards and blame intangible things beyond their control.

And so, we have to understand how we got here, to see where the problems have come from and how they have compounded. Knowledge is power, because our concerns cannot be disregarded and realities cannot be brushed to one side if we all know them to be true and can prove it, too. While there is not one person who can be blamed for our country's crisis, what is clear is that it is a build-up of multiple issues that have been wilfully ignored and left to fester for generations. Our politicians are at the forefront of this neglect because they are the people who have the ability to invest in the key pillars of our society, and so it is them whom we must hold accountable.

From the Right to Buy scheme, underfunding and stigma, to the cost of living crisis, austerity, cutting red tape and bypassing regulation, there is an amassing of issues that the government are going to need to face. What's even clearer for me now is knowing this isn't an issue that can be fixed overnight, but there are definitely things that could change immediately, such as showing willingness to solve this crisis. A willingness that clearly hasn't been there for many, many decades.

Part Two:

Neglect, Disrepair and True Stories of Lives in Crisis

Very often, change is shaped and decided upon by those at the top, those with such little understanding of what really impacts people and what could truly help them in their day-to-day lives. Politics is out of touch. Those who are in charge are not on the ground witnessing the real lives of British people. Instead, they are dictating policy from their ivory towers, and they have selective hearing for the issues they wish to target on any given day. It is because of this that the importance of grassroots activism and campaigning cannot be overstated. Driving change from the bottom will always be the most transformative in culture; it is all-encompassing and not reliant on the whims of the few. We've seen throughout human history that civil unrest and peaceful marches have an impact that can change the world. A lot of the time, grassroots activists are demonised or considered radicals or revolutionaries, but as Angela Davis said, 'Radical simply means "grasping things at the root".[1] This is why I know my contribution to this conversation and my activism is important despite the naysayers who may consider me too young or not intellectual enough. I *know* the experience of those at the 'bottom', of those who are constantly fighting to be heard and these are the people I want to highlight in this part of the book. I want to harness the collective activism of those just like me to push those at the top for change in the hope that maybe one day we could even topple these ivory towers entirely, but for now, I'm going to keep battering down the door till they hear us.

We Need to Talk About Grenfell

Trigger warning: this chapter outlines the events of the Grenfell tragedy including details of harm and death.

Everybody remembers where they were when they heard about the Grenfell disaster; I think it's fair to say it's hard to forget. For me, it was after I woke up to get ready for sixth form on 14 June between 7.00 and 7.30 am. At this point I was still living in a converted car garage in Norwood, which was our supposedly 'temporary' accommodation. We had one TV in my dad's room (if you could even call it a room) and because he enjoyed watching the news, he had left it on while he fell asleep. When I woke up in the morning to get ready, the TV was showing images of a smoking tower. I was in a morning daze, but the image shook me. From the aerial helicopter footage you could tell that the fire had been raging powerfully; not an inch of the building looked untouched by the force of it. The reporter's words fell down like a fist: 'there were reports of people trapped', 'fire engulfs West London tower', 'thirty people are taken to London hospitals'. Smoke was billowing out from the building, but I couldn't imagine anyone being stuck inside; it was just too awful to think about.

The replays of the fire from the night before made me realise how big a disaster the Grenfell fire was. My heart sank watching the fierce blaze of the fire that spread rapidly through the upper floors of the tower. It was traumatic just to see it happening through a television screen. . . seeing the footage of people on the ground screaming up at those looking out from their windows, pleading for them to get out at the top of their lungs, residents banging on their windows, many waving bits of clothes and screaming for help, chilled me to the core. Those who had narrowly escaped were shaken, wondering how the fire had spread so quickly and where the emergency services had been.

Through mobile phone footage, a timeline of what happened was pieced together from the moment the fire began in the kitchen of Flat 16. It was pure chaos, and it seemed no one was prepared for it to progress so quickly and cause so much damage. At this point, there were only whispers of deaths nothing was confirmed. Now, I've watched the news and remembered it in as much detail as when I watched the footage from Grenfell. With every minute that passed, the hope of rescuing those trapped became less and less likely. Small glimpses of hope turned into panic and despair, with residents talking of how scared they were for the many people still in the block, and how they knew the death toll was likely to be high. They could hear the screams from above but knew they couldn't help.

Running around full of adrenaline and fear asking what they should do, some considered whether they should re-enter the building and try and help people or whether they should stay outside and wait for the emergency services

– this was all while burning debris was falling to the ground around them. The overwhelming feeling watching it all play out was the sorrow for those whose homes were destroyed, whose injuries meant their lives would never be the same again, and for those who lost their lives. Knowing that they would have been confronted with the reality that they were unlikely to survive this, and what that meant for people who were young and old, in love and with families. Forced to jump, or drop your baby from a window in desperation. These are decisions that no one should ever have to make.

The days after Grenfell were painful to witness. The unbelievable scale of the tragedy was unfolding and the truth of that night was too much to bear. The gruesome details recorded by witnesses started to be shared. We heard from the individuals who had recollections of bodies piled in stairwells and by the fire escapes, of corridors filled with black smoke and no light. We learned of the families whose lives had been snuffed out, the same families who had been told by the fire services to 'stay put!' as smoke seeped into their homes. There was Khadija Saye, twenty-four years old and a talented artist with a searing passion to create. She was right on the cusp of success. There was Rania Ibrahim and her two daughters who were aged just four and three. Mohammed al-Haj Ali was the first to be identified, a Syrian refugee and a student of engineering. There was little Isaac Paulos, just five years old, who was described by his family as an 'energetic and generous little boy loved by his friends and family'. Sadness curdled into anger and pain.

Yet the number of deaths was downplayed significantly by the media, and this felt in stark disregard of eye-witness reports from the tower. The unbelievable reality of such a tragedy happening in one of the richest boroughs in the UK, and to such a predominantly working-class community, was perhaps a bit too on the nose for the media and politicians. The scepticism around the death toll was completely bizarre, with some saying it was seventeen and others saying fifty or more. It is now the general consensus, agreed by Grenfell United, that seventy-two people died in Grenfell Tower that fateful night. It was clear that damage control was enacted while smoke still spilled from the windows.

Many will remember the politicians lining the streets in remembrance of those that had died in the tower. Our then Prime Minister Theresa May visited the Grenfell site alongside politicians from all sides of Westminster, all who posted on social media with the hashtag #Grenfellforever. With promises made that things would change, many hoped these weren't empty and meaningless gestures, that you could see clearly here the brutal impact of neglect. The UK public were outraged, and many believed this event would be the catalyst for those who were most vulnerable in society. The saying 'lessons will be learned' was repeated. Consolations were plentiful. But at every stage, there seemed to be pushback for the justice the Grenfell families so clearly deserved. The regulators were not being held accountable, and neither was the cladding company who supplied the treacherous combustible material that caused the fire to progress at speed. Or those who gave them a green light to do so, despite knowing the risks.

I do wonder if the response would have been the same had a fire of this scale happened in an office block in Canary

Wharf. If it would have taken years for an inquiry to happen. Would legislation have been brought in and passed straight away to protect others working in high-rise buildings which still had illegal cladding? These are the questions I always ask myself. As the heading of this chapter says, we need to talk about Grenfell, because over seven years on from the disaster, police have only made one arrest, despite evidence disclosed at the public inquiry of what the Grenfell families claim amounts to fraudulent behaviour by companies that made the combustible materials that led to deaths. Evidence from staff working for the manufacturers of insulation materials suggests that tactics were used to make these products appear safer than they actually are, all to drive sales.[1] The deregulation and mismanagement detailed earlier has direct consequences. Yet still, tens of thousands of leaseholders remain trapped in blocks and flats which share similar fire safety defects to Grenfell tower – 111 high-rise buildings are wrapped in comparable cladding and are yet to have work completed to change this. On top of this, the *Guardian* reports that 'the government has refused to follow the inquiry's call for personal evacuation plans to be required for all disabled high-rise residents, and more than a third of fire and rescue services in England had yet to act by April this year on the inquiry's recommendation that they develop policies for scrapping "stay put" strategies if a fire spreads.'[2] I think it's fair to say, a lot of the politicians' promises were empty.

In the case of Grenfell and so many others, individuals are paying the ultimate price for corporate neglect and greed. What would these residents be doing now if they had never been taken by the fire? Maybe Khadija would be a famous artist now. If he had survived, little Isaac would be in secondary school. He'd likely be nervous about the new experience, but full of hope as young children always are. Would Mohammed have secured a career in engineering? Would he have been thankful to have found a better life in the UK? There was a young couple, Gloria and Marco, only twenty-six and twenty-seven at the time of the fire. Perhaps they'd have got married and had kids by now. For all of these people, we will never know what their lives might have looked like.

I don't want to dwell on these tragedies too much longer, but I need you to understand how real, inconceivable and *preventable* they were. If you want to read more analysis of the Grenfell tragedy, *Vice* has been covering Grenfell and the inquiry since it happened. It is also worth reading the powerful book by Peter Apps, *Show Me the Bodies*, the full story of the biggest fire in the UK since the Second World War, titled after the reply of a government official when challenged by an architect about the fire safety of tower blocks a year before the disaster.

Now there are those who are left to pick up the pieces. The homes of all those that survived had been hollowed out by the fire, their belongings destroyed. For many, all they were left with was the clothes on their backs. The days after were like nothing that I had seen before, with people donating goods, volunteering their time to help and doing absolutely anything and everything to ease the pain of these people. It was the good of humanity shining through with the community coming together in order to support those most in need. Some aid wasn't so readily available and a year on, residents were still being put up in hotels. As Muslim Aid outlined in their report a year after the tragedy, 'The time it has taken to find appropriate new accommodation or provide satisfactory arrangements for people who were evacuated or chose to leave has extended far beyond original expectations.' However, other forms of aid were potentially life-saving. In fact, the NHS recovery unit's response to the fire is said to be the biggest of its kind in Europe – more than £10 million has been spent on treatment of the mental health of those affected.[3] Many of the survivors suffered extreme PTSD, anxiety, depression and trauma following the fire. It impacted their ability to work, care for their children and has entirely disrupted their existence. The repercussions continue, and government funding only reaches so far. Thankfully, there are charity and volunteer groups, such as Muslim Aid, who have stepped in to fill the gaps and stayed helping the vulnerable with long-term unwavering support.

I was lucky enough to sit down with Ed Daffarn and Antonio Roncolato from Grenfell United to gain their views and perspective on the tragedy. Antonio lived in the Grenfell tower block for twenty-seven years and had many happy memories. His son grew up there and while there was struggle, there was a lot of love in those walls. Ed explained to me that he had happy memories too. He said, 'I love the view we had and I never understood the demonisation of tower blocks,' but he said more than this 'the most positive part was the community that became a lot stronger through hard times. You always had a chance to meet your neighbours.' And these neighbours were made up of a diverse set of backgrounds, ethnicities, religions and socio-economic differences. 'We all mucked along,' Ed shared. Ed and Antonio were a part of the bustling community and life in the tower, and while they did not lose any close loved ones in the fire, they did lose neighbours and their homes. They felt that immediately after the fire that they were 'demonised', the news outlets sharing 'rank accusations of subletting, benefits scrounging and illegal immigration, when none of it was true.' But it wasn't just following the fire they felt they were treated as inferior, but before and during the refurbishment of the building – the same refurbishment that added the dangerous cladding – they were treated like they should be grateful. Ed explained, 'If you raised your head above the parapet, they would come after you.'

They felt that in the immediate aftermath of the fire they were abandoned. Ed felt that Grenfell was a tragedy of three acts: act one was the way they were treated beforehand, with the lack of respect shown during the night of the fire; the second act was the consequences of the tragedy, the deaths and pain, and the final act was what happened in the days after. The abandonment 'by those people whose job it was to look after us.' For Antonio it took a year and a half to be allocated permanent accommodation, where he lives now. He stayed in emergency temporary accommodation for a year. But for Ed it took four and a half years to get permanent accommodation. They had tried to put him in an emergency hostel for the first night and he refused – it was a hostel with 'one room, shared bathroom and no light'. Both of them had their traumas of what happened that night. Antonio was lucky to be rescued from his flat that he stayed put in, and Ed, with a wet towel over his mouth and darkness surrounding him, fought his way to find the emergency stairwell. Blind and unable to find it, he was lucky to be found by a firefighter crawling on the ground. 'I was very lucky,' Ed told me. 'The firefighter had said it was like a one in a million shot that they found me.' And these traumas they experience live on in their lives, with both of them being hyper-aware of emergency exits in public buildings. Ed said, 'I can't look at a building without figuring out whether it's got cladding on it or not.'

Both are contributing to the motivating force of Grenfell United, helping to find a justice that should have already been served. They felt there were a multitude of structural and political reasons which led to the disaster unfolding, with journalists and media not hearing them until it was too late, and politicians having selfish desires that took precedence over actually doing good. Ed told me, 'I think one of the greatest failures of the public inquiry is that the people behind it have explicitly chosen to not look at race and class as a causative factor of Grenfell.' His thoughts also came to the location of Grenfell, in the centre of the most expensive borough in London. 'The land we lived on was a gold mine. They didn't even have to dig for the gold, they just had to remove the people living there. And then we became something that was really quite expendable. And I think that you put that commodity, the gentrification, race and class, into a thing and it's dynamite. The potential for disaster is never-ending. I've always thought when people say it's about institutionalised racism, that that is not untrue, but it's slightly more complex – that there was this issue about the land that we lived on and the value of that land, and that played an important part in the way that we were disrespected.'

When I asked them what lessons have been learned, they both professed how frustrating it is that politicians so quickly come and go, with Ed stating, 'We've had four prime ministers, we've had, I think, seven secretaries of state. No sooner do you sit down in front of one of them than another's in front of you.' The lack of longtermism and forward-thinking means that lessons may be learned in the immediate aftermath, but when some years pass, these lessons might be lost again. When it comes to housing, Antonio wants the government to 'build new homes, new houses and new accommodation' with the right policies to support this. Ed wants the culture to shift when it comes to how housing associations and landlords treat the people that live in their homes. 'We've seen so much ill treatment, disrespect. We need to have a set of people in the industry that have a proper set of ethics and values.' They also feel that the media must get behind the voice of the people: 'If it was a hospital mistreating as many people as were being mistreated on a housing estate, the journalists would have covered it.' More than anything, though, the pair, and the others at Grenfell United and beyond, seek justice for the seventy-two lives lost, and are determined to create a legacy that will remember them. It is not an easy journey, and it strikes me when Ed references Hillsborough: 'The one lesson from Hillsborough should have been that if there is a tragedy that involves a mass loss of lives again, you should never have to wait twenty to thirty years for justice. And yet we can tick many years off and we're nowhere near any form of justice.' Similarly, I think of those individuals who were failed in the Post Office scandal. It took twenty years for them to see justice served, and it took an ITV drama and widespread public awareness for the government to act.

Driving past Grenfell is hard. You pass the shell of a building that was once full and brimming with life. Today it is draped in all white with the message emblazoned across it to never forget. For me, Ed, Antonio, the other victims of Grenfell, and many others who have experienced housing disrepair and negligence, it is a haunting reminder of where systemic injustice can lead. For the government, it seems to be a dark hole in their history that they are keen to leave in the past.

Accountability, learning and change were all essential reckonings after such a critical incident, but seven years on, have any lessons truly been learned after Grenfell?

On the Front Line

You don't have to look far to find out if lessons have been learned. No other incident truly describes how bad and morally bankrupt the housing sector continues to be more than the story of Sheila Seleoane. Sheila was a social housing tenant left dead and undiscovered in her home in South London for more than two years. Even after rent on the property wasn't being paid and complaints from neighbours were being made time and time again. The skeletal remains of Sheila were all that was left of a woman who was only discovered after police forced entry into the property in February 2022. Neighbours had complained about the smell that was coming from the property and their concern for Sheila and yet nothing had been done. Gas engineers had been to the property and not been able to gain entry, and yet nothing had been done. There were eighty-nine attempts made to try and contact Sheila but no one followed up. The question for me is, why? Sadly, I have seen the reasons up close.

Over the past four years, I've spoken to thousands of tenants across the United Kingdom, many with horrible and catastrophic experiences. They are all dealing with the impact of the crisis first-hand, and all of the stigma, mismanagement, deregulation, underfunding and political neglect is impacting them directly. Many of their stories have been much more than just living in a home with a caved-in ceiling, damp and mould or an infestation of mice. These things would be traumatic on their own, but the situations I have encountered and the people I've spoken to have been going through much more than that. Like Sheila, these people have been forgotten, neglected and there has been no effort to reach them. I want you to hear their stories so that you can see the brutal realities playing out around us every day, to recognise this housing crisis isn't just a faceless entity, but real people with real pain.

Case Study One: 'I'm worried this house will kill my mum'

In 2022, I received a direct message from a lady called Anjali who lives in Birmingham. A few weeks prior to her message, I had visited Birmingham to speak to tenants living in disrepair and researching to see if the issues I was seeing in London were also happening in other cities around the UK. The images that Anjali sent through to me were absolutely stomach-churning. She had told me that she was living with her mum, and was desperate for any kind of help. After speaking with Anjali over the phone, I made the decision to go back up to Birmingham in order to visit her and to see for myself just how bad things were.

It was quite a sunny and warm day, and as I approached her home she was waiting on her doorstep for me to arrive. It reminded me of when I was on my estate and I waited for Sarah, a journalist from *ITV News*, to arrive at my house in the hope that she would be able to help. Before we even got into the property I could hear the sadness and desperation in her voice. She explained what her current living situation was like, and I could see that it was impacting her deeply. She told me that she and her mum had been living with damp and mould in their property for around ten years. At that point, I had been into many homes with damp and mould, and I had lived with it myself, but nothing could have prepared me for what I saw when I walked into their home.

You could smell the damp from the moment the front door cracked open. If you've never smelt it before, all I can say is that it is distinctive and overwhelming; there is no smell like it. For Anjali and her mum, I could only assume that they must've got used to it, but for anyone else walking into the property, it's something you'd notice straight away. And Anjali had previously had people who should have helped come to her home, including members of staff from the Birmingham City Council housing department. They would have been overcome by the exact same smell that I was walking into the property. Anjali explained to me that her mum was in the front room in a hospital bed because she was elderly and had recently suffered a stroke, which had resulted in her becoming blind. Her mum didn't speak any English, but even though I was not able to understand her, I could see her distress.

I looked around the rest of the property and every single wall and door was covered in black mould. The mould was thick enough to come off on your hand if you were to wipe it. One of the worst areas, though it is hard to even say that because it was all terrible, was the bedroom. It had a single bed in the left corner of the room, up against the wall covered in mould, with curtains growing mould and very little furniture because much of it had been destroyed. Anjali explained that she was an NHS worker who had worked throughout the whole pandemic, helping to save lives, and she explained how hard it was to work long hours every day helping others to then return home to such poor conditions. She broke down several times, explaining how she did everything she could to help people in her line of work, but when she and her mum were struggling, there was no help to be found. I continued walking around the house and then went into the bathroom which had no windows and had what looked like a sewage leak running down the wall. Again, every ceramic bathroom tile was covered in a layer of black damp mould and the one fan in the bathroom was no longer working and hadn't been replaced despite repeated requests. The bathroom door had once been white, but now it was grey and black, with smear marks from times when Anjali had tried to clean it. You could feel the weight of the damp on your chest and Anjali was incredibly worried for her mum's health as she was stuck in the living room with so little fresh air. The kitchen was so old I instantly knew it was older than me. . . and once again, the mould was festering and seeping into all corners of the room. Most of the kitchen-unit doors were missing, and it was dilapidated to say the least. I remember standing in Anjali's kitchen, five years after Grenfell, looking up at the ceiling and ceiling tiles, noticing they were made from Styrofoam, an extremely flammable and high-risk material.

The housing professionals had walked into these spaces and seen all the same things I did, and left without offering the aid so clearly required. They promised they would help, Anjali told me, but perhaps the individual that visited had communicated with someone else who hadn't followed up or they'd simply forgotten to log the issues. Maybe, they just didn't see the property, Anjali or her mum as a priority. I wanted to resolve the problem for Anjali and her mum and I needed the council to act. To live in this situation, day in and day out, had had a profound impact on Anjali's health and well-being. Nobody wants to be living in conditions like that, no matter who they are. This was and is about human decency, and it's about respect for a fellow human being. In this situation, I felt that whoever had been to Anjali's home did not have enough respect for the family, plain and simple.

Before I left I went into the front room and Anjali spoke to her mum, and beckoned me to the side of her bed. She translated for me and explained to her mum that I was a campaigner and that I was there to help them in every way I could. She immediately burst into tears, looking on imploringly. The pain, suffering and the sheer desperation that these two women were in was hard to witness. Anjali felt guilty for the condition her mum was having to live in, knowing she was helpless to change anything. These situations can impact families severely, breaking down bonds or causing significant fall-outs. I'll never forget the words Anjali spoke softly to me before I left. 'I don't want my mum to die but I think this is going to kill her.'

I'd be lying if I said hearing things like this, and handling people's pain, wasn't hard for me to manage. I am just one individual working to solve a problem so widespread it is easy to feel overwhelmed and overworked. I worry especially in the cases where I receive messages from people telling me they are suicidal, or that they have given up, that I am their last option for finding hope and that if I don't respond to their message or email that I am potentially at fault. So how do I do it? Sharing in people's suffering is the toughest thing to do as a campaigner and activist, but I have to do my best to use these experiences and stories to push me forward, rather than let them bear down on me till I also collapse. It isn't easy when the suffering is so real, and so alike to my own experiences, but I've started to come to terms with this and I understand I can't shoulder everything. I try my best to also look after myself but it's a hard balance and one that I don't think I've even got right despite being years into doing this work. Who knows if I will for a very long time to come?

Being an activist requires real self-preservation. You need to pour into yourself before you pour into others, otherwise you will have nothing to give. It's not easy to push ahead with a positive mindset and to maintain my sanity too. In some ways, being on the front line of the crisis offers a constant reminder of why I do what I do and what my purpose is. I know that eventually every storm runs out of rain, and I remind myself of that often. I'm aware that I can't make miracles happen, but I can try my absolute best for people to get them out of their current situations or make some kind of progress towards a better start. Often all they need is for someone to actually listen to them. Someone who cares and shows them that it's OK to feel how they feel, to be vulnerable and to feel helpless. All of us just want to be treated like we matter, and that we have someone on our side.

I told myself that day when I was leaving and in my cab back to the station that I was going to help this family by any means possible. If I needed to shame absolutely every single individual in the housing department at Birmingham Council, I would. These poor living conditions are not up for debate, and no matter your job title or your responsibilities, when working in housing divisions, if you see people struggling like this you should stand up and say something, not look away. You wouldn't wish such discomfort and suffering on your worst enemy, so why can so many turn a blind eye to strangers in this position?

After my post about Anjali and her mum went viral on social media, the pair were give a new property, free from the disrepair that had been plaguing them for so long. Anjali sent me videos and pictures of the garden she had wanted for so long, and I was so happy I had played a part in getting her there. More than anything though, I was happy she was safe and that she did not have to worry about the risk to her mother. It was a heavy and depressing weight lifted off their shoulders, and a place they could finally call home. It shouldn't have taken this to change things, but it highlights the pressure required for those with the power to act.

Case Study Two: 'If I speak up, they might take my kids away'

As time has gone on, the answer to the question of whether lessons were learned after Grenfell has become clearer and clearer. I didn't expect the answer to reveal itself in such a devastating way. There are no excuses for it. We have had seven years to make a change and the situation has remained stagnant. People's lives are being played with like pawns in a game of chess, where money, profit and maximum cost efficiency is given to the winner.

One of the families who highlighted to me how little had changed was the Moussokoa Palazzo family, whom I visited in 2022. Moussokoa had moved from France in 2002 to begin a new life in the UK, gaining British citizenship in 2010. For a long time she had been a social housing tenant, paying rent for the accommodation from L&Q, a housing provider, that she and her young children lived in. Her details were passed to me by a journalist friend of mine who so desperately wanted to do everything to help her and her family. I was briefed about how bad her situation was but nothing can really ever prepare you. It was late morning and my friend and I decided to look around the communal areas before heading to the property. Though incredibly run-down, there was nothing that fully gave away the brutal reality of Moussokoa's life inside. She explained how difficult her situation had been, how depressed she had become and how she felt she was being ignored by her landlord. She warned me about the cockroach infestation. Having lived with cockroaches before I thought I was mentally prepared for what I would see in her home. I later learned I'd hugely misunderstood the extent and scale of her infestation. She had told me how bad the maintenance of her communal areas had been and that several workmen had been into the property, seen the issues and after giving false promises, left, never to return. I was made aware of an ongoing leak from her boiler and that she had gone weeks without it being repaired, resulting in the water destroying much of her flat and its contents. I was told that engineers came to look but refused to deal with it because of the cockroach infestation and it posing a threat to them, and that apparently nobody would come to deal with the cockroaches because of the leak. The safety of her family was never taken into consideration. I found it astounding that you could consider a house being unsafe for engineers, but fine for a mum with young kids to live in.

She kept warning me and apologising in advance for the current condition of her home and I could see the tsunami of shame consuming her, even though none of it was her fault. It's hard to reassure someone that has been experiencing this for so long and who has had no real help so far. I didn't want to promise too much, but I was ready to see the truth of it myself. We exited the lift and right ahead was her front door, number 44. From the outside it looked ordinary. The front door even had a sticker saying 'Welcome, kick your shoes off' in large writing. She handed me the key to open the door and I did so, with difficulty. It felt as though there was a boulder up against the back of the door, and even with my full weight being thrown on to it, I could barely open it halfway. Straight away my thoughts were: *How is this fire-safe? What if a fire happened? How would they escape?* I had never experienced anything like it. Grenfell was still a fresh memory, but here I was in a building that was putting people at the same risk. The reason the front door was so difficult to open was because of the leak from the boiler adjacent to the front door. It was streaming with water.

Entering the front door, the property took the shape of an 'L' – you could continue straight ahead to the bedroom or take an immediate right towards the living room. The internal doors were also so swollen from the ongoing leak that it became impossible to fully close them. While examining the leak, which was directly above electrical switch sockets, I spoke to Moussokoa, who told me she had to switch off her washing machine – which has now been destroyed – directly below the sockets. At the back of the washing machine was a wall now covered in thick, black mould. Directly under the leak was a black bucket that she had placed there and had to empty regularly, she told me, which in itself was both a mental and physical challenge. The bucket was pretty much full when I was there and an unwanted guest was floating on its back in the water. A cockroach, the first that I had seen since being in the home.

Moussokoa believed they had been confined to the kids' bedroom, but as I already knew, these pests multiply fast and end up all over the home. At that point I thought I had seen the worst; I think for anyone that would have been more than enough to drive them insane. We began to work our way towards the kids' bedrooms, but because of the flooding, the wooden flooring had now become warped and was now a trip hazard, especially for young kids. Heading into the bedroom, she told me that this is where the worst of the cockroach infestation was.

Upon entering I didn't see much activity. She pointed out a few dead cockroaches on some shelves and next to her children's toys. I asked where the worst of it was and that is when she reached over to the mattress, attempting to pull it up but immediately let go. She let out a scream and panic, running towards the door. On the second attempt, I helped move the mattress. Underneath there were hundreds of cockroaches scuttling around under the base of the bed. They were everywhere. They were climbing up the legs of the bed and some were even on the mattress we moved, varying in size from small to fully grown, clearly an infestation that had existed for a while. This is something that Moussokoa had complained about for more than a year. Due to our interruption, the cockroaches scattered, desperately trying to burrow under anything that they could find. We left the room quickly as it was easy for me to see the extent of the problem, and Moussokoa was really shaken up. She lived with the reality these creatures were there, but being faced with them on such a scale had deeply upset her. For me, the worst part was the idea that kids had to sleep in this room every night. I worried about the trauma they would feel being exposed to these insects. We left the children's room and headed to the living room and kitchen to have another chat about what it had been like for her. I have not forgotten some of the words she said to me, and I won't for a very long time.

Moussokoa told me that she had been at the property since 2012, which at the time of meeting her had been ten years. She had been battling the issue with cockroaches in her home for more than a year. Often, the cockroaches crawled over her and her kids at night, terrifying all of them. She then went on to tell me that she had once found a cockroach buried in her ear one morning and had to have it removed. She told me about all the pesticides that she was using in her home to tackle the problem but nothing seemed to be working. I was deeply concerned when she mentioned that she had appointments with her doctor concerning her liver who believed the health issues she was having may have been because of the pesticides infiltrating her system. She was due to have a blood test that would make the real impact on herself clear, but more than anything she was scared for her children.

'My son and daughter are terrified. Mostly they sleep in my bed out of fear of the creatures underneath theirs. I'm struggling mentally. I don't even want to say anything because I don't want anybody to come and take my kids from me, but I don't sleep, I can't do anything and I'm suicidal.'

This was a mother who was at the point of collapse, yet her provider had not considered this personal impact when they walked away from her and the issues she was having at her home. And she *still* was required to pay rent on a monthly basis for these horrific conditions. The toll on her was showing as she tried to make a life for herself and her children, despite the circumstances around them. She hadn't been listened to, and now she was scared to speak up, fearing she could be blamed for it or that her young children would be taken from her. Financially, she was also seeing the impact as she had to spend her own hard-earned money to tackle some of the issues that were happening in her home, which were absolutely things that, contractually, their landlord had a duty to take care of. Luckily, Moussokoa was given a new property, although she wasn't compensated for the belongings that had been damaged.

Moussokoa's story demonstrates how often children are the overlooked victims of this housing crisis. The concerns of their parents are raised and simply ignored. This can have an extremely negative impact on their health and education. I strongly feel that many in the UK are not at all aware of the absolute poverty that many British children are living in. Some of the most eye-opening moments for me in my work have been walking into the homes of families with young children in abject poverty, fighting to make a life in the worst conditions. Many of these children are written off as badly behaved in lessons, so they quickly fall behind in their education. There is little understanding of their home life and the stresses and pressures on them that distract them entirely from the work at hand. The National Children's Bureau reports that around 3.6

million children are in poor or overcrowded homes.[1] It also states that children in poor housing are between 1.5 and 3.5 times more likely to develop a cough and are 25 per cent more at risk of severe ill health or disability.[2] These children are also ten times more likely to contract meningitis in overcrowded homes.[3] Poor housing will impact them throughout their lives too, as bad housing will often result in lower educational attainment and a greater chance of unemployment; these children are also three to four times more likely to have mental health issues.[4]

It was just over a year ago now that I was invited to meet a friend and old work colleague who was the safeguarding lead at a secondary school. She was deeply concerned for the young people at her school. She shocked me by explaining that poor living conditions were not considered a safeguarding concern in secondary schools. There is no doubt in my mind that this should change. Everything is linked, and so often teachers are the first people to notice that a child is not doing well or struggling, whether they see the child falling asleep at their desk or with a continual cough. They would be perfectly placed to instigate a conversation that might protect a child from poor housing habitation and there could be a process that is engaged that would put much-needed pressure on the housing provider.

Some schools are stepping up incredibly, despite them not having any responsibility to do so. Recently, the BBC reported on Harris Academy, a Peckham primary school where most of the children are homeless.[5] Now, as you can imagine, homeless children are even more vulnerable than those in poor housing, and this directly impacts their education. Homeless children are more likely to miss an average of fifty-five school days due to the disruption of moves into and between temporary accommodation.[6] At this school in Peckham, they have 300 students and all of them receive free uniforms, trips and meals. The school conducted a survey in which most families described themselves as living in 'non-secure tenancies' which could mean anything from sofa surfing to living in B & Bs and hostels. The principal and her teaching staff are having to pick up the emotional baggage of parents who are suffering from the lack of stability, as well as offer support to them to try and help them find secure, permanent housing so that their students can be safe. This work is beyond a job role that is already incredibly demanding. The principal, Ms Corbett, explained: 'For many of our children, they go home into a crisis situation with grown-ups who are pushed to their limits and might be suffering from depression as a result of the situation that they're in.'

One thing is clear – we are failing children in this country. Moussokoa's children, who are frightened to sleep in a cockroach-infested home, and the huge number of children homeless at Harris Academy are just two examples of a widespread problem. Since the cost of living crisis, 350,000 more children have been pulled into poverty.[7] That brings us to 4.2 million (2021–22). I always find statistics cold and too distanced, so let me just say here that those 4.2 million would fill a football stadium *seventy times*. And each of those kids represents a person with a personality and dreams, thoughts and hopes, friends and siblings – 4.2

million individuals who haven't got a safe home. These problems require a dramatic solution, and that will require a huge amount of investment, both on a personal level but also on a wider political and systemic level. There's no doubt in my mind, and from what I've witnessed, that it would be worth it.

Case Study Three: Survival of the fittest

I came across a story while writing this book that really shook me to my core, and the images of the man concerned are nothing short of disturbing. Stephen Smith, sixty-four, from Liverpool, had multiple debilitating diseases and had dropped to just six stone when he was denied benefits and deemed fit to work. He could hardly walk and was struggling with chronic obstructive pulmonary disease, osteoarthritis, an enlarged prostate and was using a colostomy bag to go to the toilet. This was a man who was not well or able by any stretch of the imagination, yet in 2017 he failed a Department of Work and Pensions (DWP) work capability assessment which meant his Employment and Support Allowance (ESA) payments were stopped. He was instead given a Jobseeker's Allowance and was required to actively seek employment. He told the *Liverpool Echo* that he lived alone and that he 'could only make it to the kitchen to make food once a day.' He added, 'I had no muscles in the back of my leg, which meant I couldn't stand up at all and had to lean or sit down all the time, but they were telling me I was fit for work.'[1] To get his benefits reinstated, he had to discharge himself from hospital, where he was being treated for pneumonia, to attend a tribunal to argue his case, which he ended up winning. The DWP eventually apologised, and Stephen received back payments of his ESA allowance. However, extreme damage had been done. Sadly, in 2019, Stephen passed away. Who knows how much of this was a result of the pressure his body was put under due to government neglect? He was let down immensely, and photos of his emaciated body is proof of it.[2]

Stephen's story is nothing new. In 2015, statistics were published that nearly ninety people a month are dying after being declared fit for work.[3] In 2018, the body of Errol Graham was found at his home in Nottingham – he had starved to death after his benefits were cut.[4] In 2014, a woman in a coma was told to find work. Another 25-year-old woman was 'repeatedly asked invasive questions about suicide' and subsequently had her Personal Independence Payment cut.[5] New academic research also reported that there were links between the UK government's harsh disability assessment system called Work Capability Assessment (WCA) and increases in suicide, mental illness and use of antidepressants.[6] The facts, statistics and truths are as plain as day, and still there is discrimination against those who are disabled, fuelled by a toxic stigma that instead of vulnerable they are lazy and a burden. They are demonised in our society where it really is 'survival of the fittest'. Poverty and disability are perceived as moral failings and the harshest punishments are inflicted on those people who are already struggling. The real moral bankruptcy lies with those in power – those in government who further entrench austerity despite it actively killing some people and leaving others destitute.

I have witnessed this first-hand. I find it hard to forget most of the tenants I meet. The extremes they are dealing with are so shocking that they remain in my mind for years after, but there was one tenant I always think about when I am campaigning, and I met him on 27 April 2022. Just like Stephen, he lives in Liverpool, is disabled and battles with mental health challenges. While I was visiting the city I got a text from him asking me to call him as he'd been struggling for years, and said he'd felt reduced to less than a human because of his treatment from his housing provider, One Vision Housing Association. As we were speaking, he told me how he lived in a tower block and for the last year had to defecate in plastic bags and throw them out as his one toilet had been broken for roughly a year. He, of course had complained about this and other issues such as the damp and mould that was growing because of a leak, yet none of it had been fixed. I received pictures of his toilet bowl, which was clearly broken in two and couldn't be used, as well as bags he was having to use due to not having a working toilet. On top of this, his shower was broken and he was therefore having to bathe himself on a daily basis in the bathroom sink. Imagine just how hard that would be for an able-bodied person and you will understand that for him it was a complete nightmare. The way he was having to live was completely degrading and you can only imagine the devastating impact it would have on the mental health of an individual who didn't have any mental health challenges prior, let alone one who did.

For me, one of the biggest failures of housing providers is the way in which they treat tenants with disabilities. Many providers have anti-discrimination policies and say they go above and beyond in accommodating those with disabilities, but the treatment of some tenants I have met has been some of the worst in all cases I have come across. I've seen those who are paralysed have leaks in their homes for many weeks, if not months, those without the ability to get downstairs be unable to leave their home due to lifts being broken for weeks and having no way to exit, as well as homes with fire-safety procedures that put disabled people at an unfathomably high risk. Those with visible disabilities are treated as inferior in many instances by their housing providers and those with hidden disabilities are treated like criminals or frauds, forced time and again to prove their disability before their complaints are even considered.

These are people who are in much more precarious situations compared to other social housing tenants, but instead of being supported, they are treated with disdain. When they then respond out of frustration, they're accused of being aggressive or unhinged in some cases. For those with mental health diagnoses, these interactions can be incredibly damaging. On 2 November 2023, the Housing Ombudsman released a report detailing an incident where a tenant killed himself after his landlord, Clarion Housing Association – who are also my landlord – failed to resolve repeated noise complaints. The landlord dismissed his pleas for help with a noisy neighbour as 'whining' and told him he could not expect silence if he lived in London. This was even after the tenant's doctor warned that the effect the noise from the upstairs flat was such that he had already attempted suicide twice. The tenant complained twenty times, but was told that no action would be taken over antisocial behaviour issues and the case would be closed after the final surveyor visit. Eleven days later, the tenant took his own life. Perhaps this issue would have been easily resolvable, but for the housing provider, it wasn't worth their time. The fact someone was pushed to take their own life because of the lack of support they received is heartbreaking.

The treatment of these people is a systemic rot that is spreading day by day. From the top down, there is less and less empathy and compassion for those who have ability requirements. Frances Ryan writes extensively about this in her book *Crippled*, a blistering polemic that doesn't hold back. She describes how extensive this animosity is and that by 2016 there were 3,700 benefits investigators, which is five times as many as those who investigate tax evasion. A fascinating difference really, when you bear in mind who is typically impacted by accusations of tax evasion: politicians, business owners and the extremely wealthy, to name a few. Ultimately, she explains that the cuts are relentless and the outlook is dismal for those who need the most help. I am floored regularly by the lack of humanity shown to disabled people. Is it so hard to extend care towards those who are different from you? It shouldn't be, and it's a damning indictment of our society if it continues.

Case Study Four: 'There was nothing the family could do'

The death of Awaab Ishak shocked everyone across the UK. He passed away in 2020 in Greater Manchester, but it was the inquest in 2022 that grabbed everyone's attention. By this time, I had already been campaigning for more than a year for housing improvements to be prioritised by the government. It did feel sometimes like I was shouting into the void, that no one was really hearing me or seeing the impact on real lives like I was. And then the news of Awaab Ishak's tragic passing hit the news, and everything shifted once more. People were talking about how neglectful the housing sector was again, but I couldn't help but feel that it was all too little too late.

I have always made it clear that this crisis is disproportionately impacting Black people, Brown people and those who are marginalised. This is partly because there are more of us in social housing; in fact, Black people in England and Wales are three times more likely to live in social housing. Around 16 per cent of white British people live in social housing compared to 44 per cent of Black British people. Interestingly, British Asians were the least likely to live in social housing, though there are significant differences within this group.[1] This reveals something clear about our society, and to me, demonstrates the lack of opportunity and institutionalised racism in this country that allows some to excel, while others cannot. The discrimination and racism within the housing sector, education sector and healthcare has been reported on and researched at length by experts, so I won't be recounting it all here. However, it's important to note this context before we discuss the life of Awaab Ishak, and the preventable circumstances of his death at just two years old.

On 16 November 2022, the coroner's report on Awaab's death was released and it provided damning evidence that he had died due to prolonged exposure to damp and mould – the same damp and mould his parents had been complaining to their housing association, Rochdale Boroughwide Housing (RBH), for years. The family even reported that theirs was nowhere near the worst on the estate. Prior to the inquest to understand why a little boy had passed due to poor housing conditions, RBH had stood firmly by their statement that the damp and mould was caused by the family's lifestyle and 'ritual bathing' habits.[2] Once again, the onus is put on the people who are vulnerable rather than the systems and structures that should help them. The family not only had to deal with their sweet little boy dying, they also had to withstand the housing association placing the blame on them. The same association admitted liability later on in the inquest. Awaab Ishak's family reported the mould from as early as 2017 and contacted the association numerous times in the lead-up to Awaab's death. There should have been steps taken to complete work to prevent the issue progressing; they should have stepped in when the flat was so clearly unfit for human habitation, but they didn't.

It was the realisation for many, I think, who have long been complaining about issues with damp and mould that the negligence of the authorities in providing assistance could have lethal consequences. For a long time, damp and mould has been treated as a superficial issue, one that is the fault of the tenants and their lifestyle, instead of something wrong with the property. This victim-blaming of tenants is discrimination in action. It is the stigma I wrote about in the first part of this book in action. Fundamentally, many of these houses have not been built with damp protection in mind. The building developers have cut corners to save money in the name of profit, and this is now wreaking havoc on thousands of families up and down the country. Awaab's story is unlikely to be the last life cut short as a result of neglectful authorities, backward policies and poor conditions.

This tragic case blatantly displayed a huge disregard for human life, in this example, a child's life. It is a flagrant disregard for their health by a provider who will claim that they follow health and safety standards. Members of staff who visited the property and saw the mould with their own eyes later claimed that they were unaware that a young child was living there, which to me never made sense because any parent would know that it's impossible to hide the existence of children in a home. Whether you like it or not, their toys are dotted around everywhere, their shoes and coats out or their baby food or nappies are clearly vis-

111

ible. The suggestion they wouldn't have noticed these things holds no credibility in my eyes. In my experience, I've come across many cases where professionals, such as teachers, doctors, nurses and social workers have written to housing providers on behalf of kids who they believe are living in dangerous conditions. It is their moral responsibility to raise the concerns they have. In Awaab's case, the coroner's report stated that in July 2020 the family showed a health visitor the mould and a letter was sent dated 9 July 2020 to RBH by the health visitor, explaining their concerns about the mould and potential impact on Awaab's health.[3] Sadly, these professionals are lucky if they even get a response from the housing association or government official, and even luckier to see action taken. The safety net has holes in it and vulnerable people are falling straight through.

Racial inequality is hard-wired into the housing industry; in fact, none of our welfare systems are entirely free of bias in all of its forms. Black people are over three times more likely to experience homelessness. The statistical report carried out by Heriot-Watt University stated that 'amongst Black people with experience of homelessness, one third (32 per cent) report discrimination from a social or private landlord.'[4] These statistics are uncomfortable but unsurprising, especially if, like me, you have first-hand experience of these prejudices. Growing up, I witnessed my dad's encounters with the local council and I saw the way in which the staff would talk down to him and treat him with disdain. There were many occasions where he would use his English name when interacting with officials to potentially create greater ease with these people whom he needed to help him. He knew, as many of us do, that to be perceived as being more 'British' or having the ability to assimilate can be the difference between being assisted or dismissed. To be considered different or 'other' was to not be worthy of their time or not to have your concerns taken seriously. I have spoken to many others who do this exact same thing when speaking on the phone. It is sad the lengths people have to go to just to inspire empathy from other human beings who are meant to be looking out for them.

Landlords of a property near to where toddler Awaab Ishak died saw refugees as 'lucky' to have a home, a report has found. The Housing Ombudsman has said that Rochdale Boroughwide Housing (RBH) had a culture of 'othering' which saw staff hold prejudices and 'lazy assumptions' about asylum seekers and refugees.[5] A former staff member at RBH told the Ombudsman that residents had complained about mould but a manager had said it was 'OK and acceptable'. There is a culture shift required in our public sector. There is a lack of cultural awareness and unconscious bias has been allowed to run riot, risking lives in the process. This isn't just about Black people, but all those who might be marginalised who deserve to feel protected by our welfare system. Surely we can all agree that everyone deserves fair access to safe housing, good education and free healthcare? Then I ask, why are we restricting the access for so many people and letting them down?

I was able to speak to Awaab Ishak's family's barrister, Christian Weaver, to get his view on this tragic case. For him, this was another tragedy, just like Grenfell, 'born out of families being ignored'. He explained that 'days before the inquest started, RBH was still holding the line that it was the family's fault.' He reaffirmed to me that 'there was no evidence of ritual bathing', and that the real sadness of the case was how preventable it was. He said he had seen comments written where people suggested that 'families should be taking more responsibility for themselves', and this is completely unfair when it comes to Awaab Ishak's case, as the family did act, and nothing was done. He told me, 'At the inquest we established two things. Firstly, that the mould at that point met the definition of making the home unfit for human habitation, but secondly, the mould in that house was of such an extent that only professional intervention could have dealt with it. So absent the landlord taking action, there was nothing the family could actually do.' So all of the time when RBH weren't acting, the family couldn't either. It wasn't just RBH the family sought help from, 'they actually sought to instruct lawyers' and RBH still said that they couldn't sort the problem. When looking at the broader picture of RBH, it was even more shocking: 'Eighty per cent of the homes owned by RBH had damp or mould. The reason they weren't treating Awaab's case with the seriousness it deserved is because that was reflective of just how their housing was.' Christian took Awaab Ishak's case pro bono, and his support for the family helped them immensely, but he did state that in most cases, the bar to accessing a solicitor and the financial cost of legal representation is set too high, so many are not able to take the legal route. The power imbalance is stark and almost impossible to stand up against.

114

Ultimately, Awaab Ishak's family were let down. There has been a shift since of course, because it always takes a tragic event to incite change. On 9 February 2023, Michael Gove announced Awaab's Law, which will force social landlords to fix damp and mould within strict time limits. This is a momentous shift, and the amendment has been made to the Social Housing Regulation Bill. On the government website they state that 'the government has already committed to a rapid review of existing guidance on the health impacts of damp and mould, followed by new guidance tailored to the housing sector, to be published by summer 2023.'[6] This is a positive move and means that landlords are to be held more accountable for the conditions of their properties, as they should be. It is an incredible legacy to leave, and there is no doubt that Awaab will save the lives of other children around the UK. With that being said, families are still struggling with damp and mould and in many cases, providers are now washing it away and painting over it as quickly as possible as a tick-box exercise, with it just returning weeks or months later.

I am incredibly grateful that Awaab's parents have agreed to answer questions for this book, and I hope they will impact you just as they have me. Special thanks to Awaab's mum, Aisha Amin, dad, Faisal Abdullah, and family friend, Fasil Farooq.

What were some of the good memories you have of Awaab?

Happy memories, good memories of him growing up as a cheeky little typical two-year-old boy who loved playing out on his bike. We would take him to the park and he would play on his bike and we loved playing football with him, kicking the ball about with him, yeah. He was just a nice, sweet little boy.

Do you believe your race and background played a role in the way you were viewed and treated by RBH?
Race and background definitely played a massive role in Awaab's story and our story, the way we were treated by Rochdale Borough-wide Housing. It came up in the inquest as well, that they blamed the damp and mould in our home on 'ritual bathing'. It left us to question in our own minds, if this had happened to another family born in the UK, would they have been treated the same way? Would that suggestion about 'ritual bathing' ever have been made?

What shocked you the most about how you were treated by your landlord?
We were surprised at the fact they showed no concern that there was a little baby in the house with us, especially when we showed them all the damp and mould around the house. We explained we thought he was beginning to be affected by the damp and mould but still nothing was done, nothing was resolved, and every time we complained we kept getting knocked back; nobody was listening to us.

Before the inquiry and coroner's report, did you always think it was the damp and mould that had ultimately caused Awaab to become so sick?
Yes, we knew it was because of the damp and mould. During the winter, Awaab would develop coughs and we kept taking him to the doctors; we would tell them about the issues and explain that

nothing was getting done. For sure we knew the damp and mould was impacting his health and we communicated that with both the housing and Awaab's doctor.

What would be your message to other families across the UK living in homes with mould and particularly with young children?

Our message would be, if you're suffering with damp and mould in your house, please go and speak with your local authority or landlord and try to get the issue resolved. Do everything you can to get out of that house, even in the worst-case situations, even if it means you're homeless. Look what happened to our son. It can happen to any other young children and even adults, so I wouldn't recommend living in a house with those conditions. Now you also have the assurance of Awaab's Law too, which means social landlords have to deal with issues of damp and mould within a specific period of time after it has been reported. Even if you have family members or friends you can stay with, do that whilst your landlord deals with the damp and mould. The priority is getting out and not living amongst it; your life is more important than staying in a house full of damp and mould.

Awaab's story has connected with so many across the country. What do you hope his legacy will be, especially with the introduction of Awaab's Law?

We hope his legacy will help save lives and hold landlords account-able for allowing tenants to live in poor housing conditions that he was living in, so hopefully no one would have to go through the suffering that we went through with Awaab. Even if it helps to save one life. . . that will be Awaab's legacy.

What would be your message to social housing landlords who still continue to fail tenants and children living in homes with damp and mould?

Our message would be, they wouldn't want members of their family or friends living in those conditions, so why would you want anyone else to live in those sorts of conditions, regardless of where they come from or who they are? It's going to leave them with long-term health problems or could lead up to their death, as it did our son. Our son passed away because of the conditions his home was in and the fact we were ignored. Also, if you continue to fail, you will end up feeling the full force of Awaab's Law.

How would you like us all to remember Awaab?

Awaab was our first child, and he brought so much love and happiness into our lives. He really loved playing with his bike and ball. We remember the times he would ride his bike down the street, laughing and having fun. His ball was always with him, and they went on many adventures together. Awaab was not just our son; he was full of love and hope. He made our hearts so happy with his curiosity and innocence. Even though he's not with us any more, we will always cherish the memories we have of him. Our love for Awaab remains strong, and we're inspired by his love for life.

Part Three:

The Domino Effect

My experiences meeting people on the front line has been intrinsic to my understanding how everything is related. It comes down to everyone's human rights, and without all of these rights being fulfilled, we cannot have a thriving society. As stated in the Universal Declaration of Human Rights, we all have 'the right to a standard of living adequate for the health and well-being of ourselves and of our family, including food, clothing, housing and medical care and necessary social services, and the right to security in the event of unemployment, sickness, disability, widowhood, old age or other lack of livelihood in circumstances beyond [our] control.'[1] It is our human right to safe housing, but it is also our right to health and medical care, social services, education and all other aspects of a welfare state.

I started off on my journey as a social housing activist, fighting for the human right to safe shelter. However, as time has gone on, I now consider myself an activist in the broadest terms. As you have seen from Part Two, it is incredibly hard to tackle housing without also looking at how it impacts children's education. Similarly, it is difficult to consider healthcare without observing the way those in poor housing are more likely to experience health issues. All of these support systems are linked, and I've called them the three pillars: we need stable, well-funded and thriving social housing, healthcare and education systems to build a high-functioning society. Without one, the rest of the pillars will fall, just like dominoes.

Reinforcing Britain's Three Pillars

The three pillars in British society consist of the NHS, education and housing. They are the foundations a fulfilled life is built on. Sadly, it is clear that the foundations for all three pillars are uneven and unstable. When you look at the broader picture like this, it can feel overwhelming and near impossible to solve. However, I believe in resolving and fixing each pillar in succession, not all at once, and I believe we need to start with housing. To me, housing puts the most strain on the NHS and education, and if you resolve it you will be well on your way to stabilising society. This priority hasn't come from nowhere. It is something that has been hypothesised for hundreds of years, and probably most significant in this conversation is Maslow's hierarchy of needs. Maslow considers needs within a triangle, with the most fundamental at the bottom, and the least at the top. There are five levels to this hierarchy, and starting at the bottom, there are: physiological needs, safety and security, love and belonging, self-esteem and self-actualisation. On that bottom level where the most important needs are listed, you will find breathing, food, water, *shelter*, clothing and sleep. Housing and shelter are fundamental to our existence, an essential, physiological need.

It is the level above this where health, employment and social ability are listed, with education being the essential route to employment and social ability. We need safe and secure shelter for us to have our needs for health and education fulfilled. If you are in housing unfit for human habitation, or in poor-quality housing, you are more likely to rely on the NHS's intervention. In 2022 to 2023, the NHS spent £1.4 billion looking after those living in poor conditions, and a huge £34 million was spent treating those living in homes with damp mould. This is a huge amount of money and is resources to just put a plaster on an infection that will continue to spread if not treated at the source. From what I've seen, I expect this figure to increase as the years go by. It isn't just physical health that poor housing impacts, but mental health also. A maintained, clear, clean and functioning living space does wonders for the mind, so the alternative is just as true: a broken, rotting, disrupted or temporary living space can worsen mental health disorders in dire ways. It's so significant that the charity Mind has a whole page dedicated to exactly this, providing resources and information to help those who are suffering in poor conditions.[1] In lockdown, all of these problems became heightened. The National Housing Federation found that poor housing caused health problems for nearly a third of Brits during lockdown. The lack of space and cramped conditions was resulting in many being unable to sleep, needing to take medication or suffering from depression or anxiety.[2] No government can expect to fix healthcare and education without first fixing housing and the conditions people are forced to live in. That's the domino effect in action. We all know that the NHS services are struggling financially and most would agree that they shouldn't have to fork out huge sums to resolve an issue which is completely avoidable.

In education, poor housing and poverty mean that many children cannot focus or succeed in school and therefore it entrenches a cycle of poverty that is near-inescapable. Seen in the example of Harris Academy in Peckham, these children are disadvantaged and distracted and they are not afforded the space in their minds to learn and thrive. Homeless children are two to three times more likely to be absent from school and children living in damp or overcrowded accommodation are more likely to miss school.[3] There is a marked difference between the academic achievement of those children who don't suffer from poor living conditions and those children who do. This is due to the fact they have less space to do homework, or their parents may be suffering from mental health issues related to their poor conditions, or they might be hungry and therefore have limited capacity to concentrate and the list goes on. Then, demonstrating how clearly linked all these sectors are, the negative impact on the health of these children due to the living conditions can limit neurological and intellectual development. Not only are these children more likely to stay in poverty and poor conditions, their lack of education translates to poor productivity and this impacts economic growth in the UK. This feels like a distanced and transactional way to put it. For me, I think of all of the creative, brilliant, engaged and diverse minds who are not given the opportunity to shine and whose work we will never know.

By focusing on the *cause* of instability in our society, we then have a clearer path to follow to resolve our issues and rebuild. I believe in utilising Maslow's hierarchy and zoning in on housing, making this our priority for the political agenda while looking at the wider picture and acknowledging how we can fix many different areas at once. Prioritisation does not mean neglect, and I believe pressing issues within healthcare and education should not be abandoned to deliver on housing improvements. However, I do believe the most significant change comes from treating the rot at its root.

A Vicious Cycle

I've always been a visual learner, and in order to see an issue clearly I have to visualise it. This means the way in which I view housing is quite different to other people. Others may see housing as being separated out into different clear-cut areas such as the private rental sector, home ownership and social housing. For me, I see it in its totality. For as long as I've been campaigning in housing it has felt like the parts worked in order to make sure that the wheel continues to turn, but the wheelhouse is broken in several different areas and no one is acknowledging this as it seems everything is working OK. Our system of handling problems has always been lacking analysis, focus and drive, and by not fixing the larger-scale problem of housing we aren't resolving systems for longevity. Continuing with this wheel idea, I'd like to use a metaphor of a bicycle wheel to describe how I visualise the housing sector as working. I believe the metal frame is social housing. If the tyre of the wheel bursts, you have a stable metal framework to stop the bike from completely caving in, and wheels are replaceable, they can be built again. The rubber tyre might be private rental or property ownership. Social housing acts as a massive safety net in case anything does go disastrously wrong while also providing homes to many vulnerable individuals who don't have the capacity or ability to work. Social housing is there so that if at any point someone needs it, they can be sure to have a roof over their head.

In the 1920s, private renting dominated the housing landscape. Back then, social housing wasn't something that the government had considered prioritising; instead they had workhouses, similar to prisons, which were the last resort for the poorest in British society. The people who ended up in these institutions would be expected to work twelve-hour days in exchange for daily meals and shelter, though the conditions that were described were appalling. Some say this was done on purpose in order to disincentivise people from using them. In all periods of history, the poor have been demonised, and there have always been programmes to stop them becoming a 'nuisance'. In November 2023, we learned of Suella Braverman, then 'Home Secretary', proclaim that being homeless was a lifestyle choice, and that legislation should be brought about to destroy tents used by homeless people on our streets. It was only days later a video went viral of a dozen homeless rough sleepers having their tents, filled with belongings in some cases, thrown into the back of bin lorries.

It wasn't until after the First and Second World Wars that initiatives were started in order to build homes fit for heroes – inspired to build new communities to be safe following two fearsome wars, as well as a response to the fact that so many homes across the UK had been destroyed and with the condition of existing properties being so poor. And so, private rentals increased as the government agreed to subsidise costs for private organisations to build homes, and it was unlikely any individuals would be able to do so themselves. As the decades continued, the use of private rented accommodation by a number of landlords increased. It is an expanding option, but one that benefits very few. And, of course, we have home ownership, which was once attainable for many and has now become harder and harder, especially over the last few decades due to the increase in deposits, inflation and interest rates. When your own home is purveyed as the highest form of representation of an individual's success, what does that say about the millions who rent? Are they not successful?

For me, all of this history and facts about housing speaks to an area of our society where there has been no consistent or thoughtful strategy. We've digressed for generations from the fact that housing is unicity and a universal and foundational human right to it being an opportunity to make money and profits. All humanity has been sucked out of it. And what are we left with? Around 1.4 million people across the UK waiting for a social housing property. I've always said that wherever there's a crisis there's an opportunity to exploit, with housing being seen as an opportunity to make money rather than a necessity. Living in poor conditions is not a 'lifestyle choice' as stated by Suella Braverman recently, it is a result of a problematic cycle that is unforgiving and unrelenting.

Land hoarding also has a huge part to play here, too. In the UK it has become a significant problem, with development companies buying up acres with the promise to build homes for the many Brits who are so desperately waiting for access to them. What's happened, though, is an accumulation of 1 million plots of land being bought by development companies who haven't begun building because instead they want to wait for land value to increase in order to maximise profits. Their excuse is that they need a constant pipeline of land in order to stay afloat, but the reality is that even if they were building at a constant rate, it would take more than eight years for them to run out of land.

And so, the wheel continues to turn, but the damage is extensive and could mean there is no safe journey back. Between 2021 and 2022, there were more social homes knocked down and demolished than were built, meaning an even further deficit in the supply of social homes available to the many who are waiting. There were 18,881 social homes sold off, with 2,757 social homes demolished in the same year. This is compared to the 7,500 social homes that were built during this time frame, which in total means that there was a net loss of 14,138 social homes.[1] This lack leads those who have no other option into private renting, at risk of slum landlords and private landlord exploitation. The demand also incentivises competitiveness. There are now many people who bought up houses between 1990 and 2010 who have a vast portfolio that is making them serious money, often enough money to not need to work again. Many of these people will state they worked hard and pushed themselves to reach this position, and I am not here to blame individuals for taking opportunities that were available to them. However, I am amazed that often these same individuals don't take any moral consideration of the tenants they rent to or their circumstances.

Now what we've been seeing throughout 2023 at the time I write is an ever-increasing worry about mortgages and in particular, mortgage repayments due to repeated increases in interest rates. Increased interest rates have meant that those on fixed mortgages and variable mortgages will see their monthly costs of repayment inflate significantly, and this has even been made more difficult as a result of the ongoing cost of living crisis. Many in the UK are financially worse off than they were a few years ago. The worry about this is if things continue to get worse, it could have drastically negative repercussions on the housing sector as a whole. If those repaying their mortgages can no longer afford the monthly repayment costs, it means they will default and, in some cases, have their property repossessed. It'll pretty much be impossible for them to take out another mortgage on a property, so they will have to turn to the private renting sector. This can only mean an increase in demand for private rentals.

I've noticed the terminology used by politicians in regards to housing and it shows a clear disparity in their attitudes between renters and homeowners. The turmoil happening with mortgages and high interest rates in the UK is shocking, and it's been described as an attempt by the government to wreck people's 'secure futures'. But why is it only believed that you can have a secure future when owning your home and why is it that millions of renters aren't allowed to have the same level of security? To me, there's been a lot of theatrics around the mortgage crisis in the last few months and it's enraging considering that for so long, private renters have suffered similarly and are suffering more so now as landlords up the rent to pay for the rise in mortgage repayments. There has been little talk on the impact this is having on renters, which to me speaks louder than anything when it comes to the divide in class between renters and homeowners. You're seen as second-class citizens as renters in comparison to those who are privileged to own their own homes. And it is a privilege now the average house price is sixty-five times greater than it was in 1970, but wages are only thirty-six times higher. Indeed, prices rose by 10.9 per cent, or £27,000, in the year to February 2022 alone. The data shows that the number of those getting family help has doubled since the turn of the millennium. Among those who purchased their first home between 2015 and 2019, half (54 per cent) say they had some form of financial help from their parents. Among the most recent buyers (2020 onwards), 24 per cent say they had help with their deposit from family, including 6 per cent who had the entire deposit paid for them, and 16 per cent whose family contributed to it.[2] This is an inaccessible step up for most, and ensures that only the most stable and the 'haves' continue to have, while the have-nots are left behind.

With rental costs already extremely unaffordable in the private sector, more people coming to the private rental market could potentially push prices up even further, and in fact, some estate agents have been exploiting this, facilitating bidding wars for properties and suggesting you can win a property by paying more per month to rent. It's very much a catch-22 problem, because if a landlord can't afford their repayments, they could lose their home and ultimately, the tenant will be evicted. Or they can increase their tenants' rent, but if it becomes unaffordable for the tenant, they may end up being evicted anyway. For many that currently have mortgages, even the idea of privately renting would be too expensive. What is the solution that's left? You must know what I'm going to say by now! There that cycle goes again. This clearly demonstrates that when the private sector and home ownership fail, the automatic default is to turn to social housing.

Stealing Our Homes?

Over the last two years working as a housing campaigner, I've had the pleasure of working with a huge variety of different people, including those that have come to the United Kingdom seeking asylum. If there's one thing I hate equally as much as the stigmatisation of social housing tenants, it's the stigmatisation and treatment of migrants, refugees and asylum seekers. There is no doubt that those coming to the UK for refuge have been demonised and used as a weapon or political football within our country, and scapegoated as our crisis escalates. I often see them being blamed for coming here and stealing our homes, taking our jobs, or scrounging off the government. In fact, in January 2024, it was revealed that the Conservative party plan to release a scheme to provide 'British homes for British workers', furthering the far right rhetoric that we are inundated with 'foreign invaders'. This is another deflection tactic from the Conservatives, to avoid taking responsibility for the problems this country faces. While the Conservatives said this was speculation, it's very on brand for them.[1] None of these claims are rooted in fact, and the scale of any issues that refugees may cause has been inflated and escalated through ignorance. So I do want to use this opportunity to explain the reality of what happens when those fleeing persecution, war, violence or discrimination come to the UK in order to settle. I believe it is far different to what many think and proves that their lives aren't made as easy as some may have you believe. I see these people as victims within this domino effect – pulled in on empty promises and then becoming neglected and exploited and, realistically, they are just as vulnerable, if not more so, than British-born people in poverty in many instances.

I've worked with a victim of gang violence and FGM (female genital mutilation) from Kenya, who fled and was forced to leave her kids behind. She told me she was going to be killed. Her infection as a result of the FGM was so bad that when she reached the United Kingdom, she needed immediate medical treatment. She showed me the scars on her legs after a machete was used on her by the gang, and pictures of her face and body, black and blue and almost unrecognisable after being mercilessly beaten by her husband. Her brother and sister were murdered by the same gang and her father's home had been burned down and destroyed several times after she left and fled to the UK. She showed me the video of her sister being violently beaten by them while naked in a field. Hours later, she was discovered dead, having been abandoned there. It is these stories that are often lost in the depersonalisation of refugees. I've also witnessed the struggle of Afghan refugees who arrived in the UK after escaping the Taliban invasion in Afghanistan. Staying home would have meant they would be killed. Most didn't want to come to Europe, and would much rather have stayed in the place of their birth, where their culture and tradition originated from. They are left without a choice and are grateful for opportunities to find safety abroad. I've also spoken to asylum seekers who arrived in the UK when they were young kids, but more than a decade later are still waiting for asylum to be granted. There is so much diversity within these stories that I have heard, but what I want to emphasise here is that, for the vast majority, their shared story is trauma, fear and a hope for survival.

When you arrive here in the UK and seek asylum, you are not automatically given keys to a social housing property. Instead, when you get here you are housed by the Home Office in accommodation provided by one of their contractors or you and your family will be placed in a hotel, hostel or bed and breakfast. The word 'hotel' might sound luxurious, but in fact, it's quite the opposite as these refugee families tend to be crammed like sardines into one room and treated and processed like prisoners. In regards to the accommodation provided by the Home Office's contractors, the conditions are terrible, with many homes in a state of disrepair. These asylum seekers have no option but to take the accommodation provided to them and be grateful for it, no matter the condition. They will continue to live like this until their asylum application is processed and either granted or denied. At a minimum this can take a few years, and that's if you're lucky; for many, it can take decades. This leaves them in a painfully precarious position, unable to place stable roots in communities or create safety and security for their children. There is no red carpet rolled out for them or a life of luxury granted when they enter the UK.

If you do, however, end up having your asylum application granted, you are asked to leave the accommodation provided by the Home Office and told to find your own. In some cases this could be private accommodation, but in many cases, due to the short turnaround time after your asylum application has been granted, it means that they will need to depend on the help of the local authority because they are unaware of how housing works in the United Kingdom. In many of these cases, the local authority would advise that these individuals move into the private sector and rent due to the shortage of social housing properties. This isn't affordable for everyone, and the alternative is to place these people in temporary accommodation, joining the millions on the social housing waiting list. The conditions of these temporary accommodations vary, but in a lot of cases there is significant disrepair and no desire or incentive to improve conditions. There is nothing 'temporary' about temporary accommodation and families live like this for many, many years.

The suggestion that migrants are prioritised above Brits when it comes to social housing is completely wrong, too. There's a whole host of provisions and conditions within the legal framework, and it would be unlawful to bring in a policy that prioritises migrants over indigenous households. Therefore, local authorities cannot provide housing to former or current asylum seekers over British nationals who are seeking social housing. Eventually, depending on their need, these individuals may be moved into permanent social housing, but again this varies by need.

Education and awareness are incredibly important to prevent the demonisation of refugees in the UK and to disprove the dangerous political rhetoric that there is an 'invasion' of migrants coming to our shores.[2] It has always been the case that people would migrate around the world or move locations due to famine, disease, war or climate disaster; it is nothing new. However, while the number of refugees has increased due to forced displacement, this can be down to a number of wider factors, including population increases and climate change. The UK does not have more refugees than most other countries – there are far greater numbers of forced migrants in France, Germany, Spain and Italy. According to statistics from the United Nations High Commissioner for Refugees (UNHCR), as of November 2022, there were 231,597 refugees, 127,421 pending asylum cases and 5,483 stateless persons in the UK. The war in Ukraine drove a large increase from the previous year.[3] This equates to just 0.54 per cent of the UK population.[4] Altogether, 10.6 million people across the UK are living in social housing, but of that only 161,000 people (that's 1.5 per cent) arrived in the UK within the last five years. Only 15 per cent of those living in social housing are foreign-born, including those who have citizenship.[5] Also, '90% of the lead tenants in social housing are British citizens.'[6]

In 2023, the prime minister made stopping the boats one of his five promises to the British people. The 'Stop the Boats' Bill has the aim to end illegal entry as a route to asylum in the UK. The so-called compassionate root of this bill is to disincentivise people from risking their lives through dangerous journeys and prevent criminals from profiting from this human trafficking. These people, who will have risked so much and will be incredibly vulnerable, will be detained and taken back to their home countries or to another safe third country, such as Rwanda. This is a drastic and unbelievably unfair policy to introduce for such a small number of people who are simply seeking safe refuge. Politicians are utilising the lives of migrants to create polarisation, divide people and create scapegoats and we should acknowledge that this has long been a strategy of those in power. Suella Braverman is someone who is pushing for this in a big way, despite the fact that her parents themselves were migrants who travelled from Kenya and Mauritius to come to the UK. The idea that a 'resolution' would be carting off these people to a country unknown to them, such as Rwanda, is a real show of Western power-play and delusion, using a colonised African country as a pawn who has little to no say. This is without the fact that over the last few years there have been high tensions between Rwanda and the Democratic Republic of the Congo with talk of potential all-out conflict.

These migrants have also been described as criminals and organised gang members. The fact that these comments and notions have been peddled by the government means that many do consider refugees to be dangerous. However, it has to be noted that this isn't the case when we speak of Ukrainian refugees, the number of which has risen most significantly in the past few years. As well as this difference in perception, we've seen the many millions that the government has provided not only to help Ukrainian refugees but also to the Ukraine in general. This is easily contrasted to the treatment of Afghan refugees in the UK. The only difference between these people who have come here is the colour of their skin and the country that they are from. I believe that different refugees are discriminated against because of their skin colour and culture. Also, in regards to the idea that asylum seekers are coming to the UK and stealing people's jobs or scrounging off the government, the truth is far more stark. When refugees arrive in the UK they have no recourse to public funds, including work. As a result this means that they are expected to live on £35 per week.

Many of the people who currently live in the United Kingdom have parents and grandparents who were immigrants; people who moved to the United Kingdom for various reasons, including fleeing persecution or simply to create a better life for themselves and their families. In their time here they have contributed massively to the UK economy, tax system and culture. Both my parents did this, as did the parents of so many others. Just one look at our sports teams will demonstrate this point. Take the contributions of Sir Mo Farah, who came to the United Kingdom as an asylum seeker and went on to win multiple international medals and Olympic medals for Great Britain. Although his successes are exceptional, most asylum seekers do contribute to life in the UK in positive, yet smaller ways. Other famous refugees include Freddie Mercury, the lead singer of the beloved band Queen; singer Rita Ora; Victor Moses, the football player for Chelsea, Liverpool and West Ham and Momtaza Mehri, a former Young People's Laureate for London.

There is a dark side to not allowing asylum seekers to work here in the UK; not only does it make our society more stagnant and less rich in culture and difference, it also leaves us poorer financially. Migrants and refugees have been foundational for our welfare services and allowing them to thrive. Immigration is good for the NHS and the migrants who come here provide vital services. We currently have a shortage of 40,000 nurses, a shortage that could be supplemented by migration.[7] If asylum seekers coming here aren't allowed to work, it can push them to seek work illegally, and they are often exploited as a result of this. If we dramatically shifted our thinking around migrants and refugees in the UK, we could see really positive moves in our culture, economy and welfare. As Zadie Smith said, 'The hardest thing for anyone is accepting that other people are real as you are. That's it. Not using them as tools, not using them as examples or things to make yourself feel better or things to get over or under.'[8] Let's accept refugees and asylum seekers as real people, and give them every grace that humanity should offer, rather than letting them become the scapegoats for a system that is failing for many reasons that don't involve them.

Crime and Domestic Violence

Nobody really talks about the impact of housing on the level of crime in the UK. Like many things, it's often not even considered as an interlinking issue or part of the falling dominoes of our welfare state, but when you think about it deeply, it absolutely makes sense. I've spoken to families who have committed crimes in order to earn extra income, whether to pay rent, fix issues in their homes or feed themselves and their children. There are young kids who feel that they have a responsibility to help their parents or feel under pressure to keep up with their friends who have more money – or appear to – and they turn to crime in order to make money. The poor state of housing here in the UK disproportionately affects those from poorer backgrounds and our welfare system, and instead of acting as a safety net, is leaving people in disrepair, neglected or is casting them out altogether. Those who might have to consider private renting due to the lack of social housing supply might be under pressure to keep up with rent, so in order to pay it off they look to fast and illegal means to make a quick buck. Crime rarely happens out of the blue. It is the result of poverty, unemployment, abuse, neglect, poor conditions, addiction issues and mental health disorders. This is not to say that people aren't culpable, but is to emphasise that socio-economic conditions and our environment play massive roles in either worsening or abetting crime rates. Rising crime is a damning indictment of the state of a country and the UK's crime rate was 4 per cent higher in 2023 than the previous year.[1]

The idea of crime being an individual's active choice and not a result of any external factors only serves those who don't want us to see that our support systems are on their last legs. For example, the cost of living crisis has increased shoplifting, with police forces in England, Wales and Northern Ireland recording nearly 33,000 incidents of shoplifting in 2023, a significant 30.9 per cent increase compared with March last year.[2] Violent crime sits in a different category, of course, but we do know that such violence can be worsened when many people feel disenfranchised and are struggling in a variety of ways. A flourishing support system could reduce the amount of petty and violent crime, if those struggling have better access to mental health support, opportunities for education or employment and have access to safe, stable housing.

Domestic violence is another issue that regularly appears among social housing tenants and I have experienced countless situations of women reaching out in fear as they have been victims of domestic violence. Housing options are so limited that for many women and men it may feel that they are trapped in a situation with their abuser. Often, domestic violence victims will seek help from their local authority or housing association and, as a result, be moved into temporary accommodation. In many of these cases, these individuals are either struggling to get help from their housing provider or have been placed in terrible conditions far different from where they were living before. Some even consider moving back in with a partner who has abused them so that their children can have safe and stable living conditions. Women have reached out to me and revealed they have been moved into hospitals or hostels with drug addicts and are fearful because needles have been left around and there are no locks or safety measures in place. Women's Aid lists 'practical reasons' as a key reason women don't leave a violent situation, and the instability of housing falls within this.[3] Perhaps they are moved to a location riddled with disrepair that has damp and mould, infestations of mice and is overcrowded, and when they are in such a vulnerable position anyway, this feels like a huge failure of duty of care from local authorities and social housing providers. What this often means is that these women feel trapped in a cycle of domestic violence, or feel as if they have moved from a bad situation into another bad situation.

As our prisons fill up and reach bursting point, with 98 per cent of available spaces full, there needs to be a refocus of priorities onto policy and investment that reduces crime rates, rather than a system that just punishes once the crime happens. Proactivity and getting down to the root cause has been a focus throughout this book, and in serving and protecting the needs on Maslow's hierarchy, investing in housing and the foundations of welfare could prevent crime before it ever has the chance to manifest.

What Happens When We Have a Lack of Homes?

Overcrowding has become one of the biggest issues caused by the housing crisis, and after I took a trip to New York early in 2023, I realised this isn't just a UK-wide issue but one that is prevalent in many developed cities across the world. Compared to the average European country, Britain today has a backlog of 4.3 million homes that are missing from the national housing market because they were never built. This overall housing deficit would take at least half a century to fill, even if the government's current target to build 300,000 homes a year is reached. This has therefore created a heightened demand for space, and resulted in landlords carving up houses into smaller and smaller portions to fit in as many people as possible. There are many situations where properties have had their living rooms converted into an extra bedroom to try and accommodate a family, or there will be six to eight people to a house, with one shared bathroom and kitchen. At its worst, I have seen a room to rent advertisement where a bed was put into a bathroom, and *that* was deemed a suitable room for someone to reside in. If you're in council housing or your house is owned by a housing association, you're entitled to a bedroom for every person over sixteen years old (eighteen years old in Northern Ireland) and every married couple so you shouldn't need to share a room with your child. The key word here is 'entitled'. To be entitled to something doesn't necessarily mean you will ever get it. Overcrowding is inevitable in our current housing climate, and this is leading to more and more problems.

It isn't just overcrowding that happens when we have a lack of housing available, of course, but this extreme lack leads to widespread homelessness as many who can't afford private rent or can't access social housing are forced to sleep on the streets instead. Rough sleeping is a direct result of housing inequality in the UK. It is perhaps the most extreme form of homelessness that anyone could face. New figures released by the Combined Homelessness and Information Network (CHAIN) in 2023 showed a sharp rise in rough sleeping across London, with over 10,000 people recorded as sleeping on the streets of the capital in the last year – an increase of 21 per cent compared to 2021–22.[1] In fact, at the time of writing, news was broken by Daniel Hewitt that the number of children living in temporary accommodation in England had increased to 138,000, an increase of 7,400 in three months. These figures highlight the impact of the cost of living crisis, which is pushing more households to the brink. With 26 per cent of those new to rough sleeping previously living in private rented accommodation, it's clear that soaring rents and a growing shortage of genuinely affordable homes is forcing more people into homelessness. This is severely exacerbated by the fact that housing benefit remains frozen at 2018–19 rent levels. Those who are rough sleeping often have additional needs, whether that be mental health, physical health or ability needs, and many of them suffer from addiction. Often these issues are neglected, and not enough support is put in place for these individuals to stabilise and perhaps rehabilitate. Over a third (35 per cent) of those sleeping rough had one or more support needs, with over half (51 per cent) of those sleeping rough having mental health needs.

One message that I think most of us need to remember is that we are always closer to being homeless than to becoming a billionaire. Even becoming a millionaire is a long way off for the majority of us. Realising this is important to promote class solidarity and to prevent demonisation of those who are rough sleeping. It's easy to think 'that could never be me', but the oppressive nature of this government, extreme overcrowding and under-resourcing of our social housing and the realities of rising costs means that you could be forced to sleep rough, though I pray for you that is never the case. I always say that housing has a massive impact on absolutely every member of British society, whether you own your own home or you're sleeping on the streets; these problems are relatable. It doesn't take much to slip through the cracks in the system, and I know that if each of us were struggling we would hope that someone was there to catch us. But that's simply not the reality.

The fact that we have one of the richest economies in the world, but an ever-rising rate of homelessness raises serious questions. Daniel Lavelle, in his book *Down and*

Out, aims to answer some of these questions, and his book rages against a system that has resulted in 274,000 homeless people in the UK (2021).[2] He details the stories of people who have, despite all their hopes for life, found themselves homeless. Daniel understands that ending homelessness is well within our means and I'm with him; in fact, during the coronavirus pandemic, it was reported that 90 per cent of homeless people were placed in safe accommodation to protect them.[3] So why can't this be in place for the longer term, too?

When it comes to real stories of people experiencing homelessness, I always come back to Karen McBride. Karen McBride was a poverty campaigner from the north of England and a mum of four who actively campaigned for reform to the benefits system, as she experienced first-hand how difficult the process of claiming benefits was here in the UK. She became homeless because the landlord of her previous property decided that they wanted to sell and as a result, Karen had to leave and find somewhere else to live. After declaring herself homeless, she was at last accepted on to the waiting list for social housing and was offered accommodation by a housing association. The conditions were described as so bad, it was deemed not fit for human habitation. Upon moving into the property, Karen realised there was no working gas or electricity in the property either. Karen's daughter, Codie, listed a range of serious defects at the house, including black mould – which made them ill and caused black dirt to come out of their noses – and pigeons nesting in the loft. The property had a live wire hanging from the master bedroom ceiling; damp in two of the three bedrooms; a wall 'thick' with black mould; a hole in the floor where 'you could see through to outside'; a leaking roof; a leaking boiler and a bird trapped in the chimney, the inquest heard. I'm sure that if anyone was offered a home in the same condition this property was in, nobody would for a second think it would be a place they were willing to accept or live in. It's interesting what is seen as acceptable when you happen to be a working-class social housing tenant, compared to other social classes in the UK. This was all after Karen was placed in various hotels and hostels when she was made homeless.

Between the threat of homelessness and sleeping rough with her children, and the lack of aid and support, Karen felt helpless and saw no way out. In August 2022, Karen tragically took her own life. The coroner ruled that this was not a case where the state or its agents had 'failed to protect the deceased against a human threat or other risk'. However, the family pointed out that the failure of multiple agencies had been contributing factors in why Karen ended up taking her own life. It's important to state here that Karen was told if she decided to turn down the property she was being offered, she would then be deemed as making herself intentionally homeless and would not be supported. Just imagine for a moment being in that situation where you're offered a property and the only property that you can afford or have access to is unsafe, disgusting and in complete disrepair. As much as you want to turn down the property, the alternative is rough sleeping with your four children. Karen's story shows how easy it can be to fall through the gaps and end up making an almost impossible choice. This is why housing reform is so essential. I believe nobody should be put in a position like Karen was.

If this story isn't enough to persuade you, then perhaps the knowledge that between 2019 and 2020 the bill for homelessness was around £1.2 billion of taxpayers' money might. It is said that if 40,000 individuals in England alone were prevented from homelessness in the space of a year, it would save UK taxpayers around £370 million. It therefore becomes difficult to understand why more isn't being done in order to prevent an issue that has become so expensive, and expensive for all of us. However, for me this is a lesser reason than the overwhelming moral and humanistic one. Everyone should have access to safe shelter, full stop.

Social Stigma Continued

Now, I know I've mentioned stigma before, but it's worth raising again a key domino effect of a lack of investment in housing and oversubscribed housing falling into disrepair. It wasn't that long ago that there wasn't much stigma attached to social housing. My grandmother told me that in her early years it wasn't seen as a bad thing, but rather a necessary part of life. The tone has shifted and there is deep-rooted disdain for those who rely on any welfare of the state – apart from the NHS – but even then there's only some who are deemed worthy enough to be using it. This bias many hold towards those in social housing and who come from lower socio-economic backgrounds can be conscious and unconscious, but in every way it is damaging and unfair. It takes away individuals' humanity and instead sees them as belonging to a wider group. We know from history what generalising can do and how it can breed hatred. It needs to be resisted at all costs.

Stigma plays a significant role and is both reactive to regressive policies around social housing as well as the causation of such policies. If we believe social housing tenants are inferior, then those impoverished are inferior, so we don't believe that anything will change or even that these people have a right to something better – it becomes a self-fulfilling prophecy. This stigma becomes incredibly problematic when the same people working to support those in social housing or supplying the housing in many cases have distaste for people using such housing. There have been a lot of cases where tenants have received poor treatment from employees, been discriminated against or stigmatised. The case of Awaab Ishak was a prime example of this. The parents of Awaab Ishak were told they should feel lucky and grateful that they were in social housing, and as immigrants, should be the last to complain about the way in which they are living. Whether it is directly or indirectly, these statements suggest that for one, Awaab Ishak's parents were undeserving of this housing, and two, that they have no right to complain or speak up. This undermines their humanity. The overlap of race and class discrimination feels the most pressing to resolve, however it isn't just people of colour who are treated in this way. There is a hierarchy when it comes to tenants and landlords in this country and that creates a power imbalance where people feel unable to speak up, or are encouraged not to, as it would disrupt the status quo. I think this power imbalance is what some professionals have used to their absolute advantage when making decisions that ultimately dictate how people live. Working in housing is seen as a business transaction, and the powers wielded over their consumers are nothing short of corrupt.

Whether they choose to admit it or not, narrative and stigma are often driven by government policies or attitude, especially towards lower classes. We have grown up with the idea that anything the government says must be informed or without question. As I've grown into my campaigning work, it's become concerning how we as the general public don't question government attitude and rhetoric more. For example, once upon a time, social housing was seen as something to be proud of by the government, along with the welfare state, and now it is seen as a burden. After the war years, the Labour Party envisaged a society where all citizens would be free from poverty and ill health. In 1942, the Beveridge Report, titled 'Social Insurance and Allied Services' was published. The man who wrote this report, social economist William Beveridge, had been drawn to the idea of remedying social inequality while working for the Toynbee Hall charitable organisation in East London. He saw that philanthropy was simply not sufficient in such circumstances and a coherent government plan would be required to battle against the 'five giants': idleness, ignorance, disease, squalor and want.[1] The report was a determination to make our society better, factoring in the long-term costs of doing so. It suggested this was some of the most important work a government could do in order to produce not just a successful labour force but a flourishing economy. The Beveridge Report listed 'squalor' as one of the 'five giants on the road to reconstruction'. It's quite scary that even after eighty years we're still calling for the same changes in quality of housing. Over time, we have lost this determination and energy to resolve our crises, and instead of looking to tackle the five giants, there are many who simply label and stigmatise the lower socio-economic classes as idle, ignorant and wanting. This is a symptom of individualism too, where capitalism sets each of us in competition rather than seeing that a rising tide raises all boats.

The government's stigma of social housing tenants and the lower classes furthers the general public's view. The public form their opinions based on policies the government wants to implement, and we've seen this fluctuate from the introduction of social housing in the 1940s to the twenty-first century where social housing is viewed as a representation of failure. In my personal opinion, the general public can't fully be blamed for their biased opinions as they are fed the information that tends to be skewed one way or another. Opinions will always be fluctuating and fickle which is why I think we need to lean much more heavily on facts. Many don't know the facts and inarguable truths. I wonder, if you were to ask members of the general public whom they think of when they hear 'social housing tenant', what they would say. I imagine it wouldn't be key workers or individuals working in the private sector. It would likely be those who are claiming benefits and refugees. There are many who would consider those in social housing to be exploiting Britain's resources. To me these are all stereotypes and generalisations, with many assumptions and biases being completely factually incorrect.

Bias is something that is indiscriminate, and sadly, we all hold it in some shape or form. Seeing bias from social housing tenants themselves does happen and, to me, is one of the saddest forms of stigma. I say this through lived experience but also from speaking to thousands of social housing tenants in my time. Some feel ashamed and like they are a burden; others consider themselves to be better than other social housing tenants, for example if they are not paid benefits or living off welfare in that way. Many say that they are grateful, no matter the situation they are in, believing they are lucky to be in social housing. What this has done is create fear among tenants up and down the country, especially when it comes to challenging authority or advocating for what they deserve. A number of the tenants I have spoken to have said to me that they at some point questioned how much they could complain about an issue without getting themselves in trouble. We know that their concerns are warranted and that there is a possibility of tenants being evicted from their homes if they complain. There is anxiety that they may fall victim to revenge eviction or perhaps another sort of punishment from their provider. Stigma and stereotyping makes people isolated and feel that they have no voice. The pervading attitudes sink into tenants' sub-conscious and makes them believe they are the issue, or that they are above the issue for some reason or another. This is not healthy and it allows for stigma to continue.

Due to stigma, providers would rather blame the tenant as opposed to looking at the actual issue through a clear lens and determining the problem. Amplified by the fact that many social housing tenants are lower class, of Black, Asian and ethnic minority heritage, disabled or other marginalised identities, the idea that these people are inferior is supported by other social biases. There needs to be significant change for those in power to start seeing these people as individuals.

Climate Change and the Environment

Climate change is a huge and more recent issue which has begun to threaten social housing and housing in general in the UK. It's been made clear by experts that we are to experience forty to fifty years of climate change whatever we do now or in years to come to reduce our CO_2 emissions. In the last year alone, we've seen record temperatures and extreme weather across the country, and the three regions of London, the East and South-East of England are likely to see the most dramatic impact.[1] In the summer of 2022 we saw temperatures in the UK hit above 40 degrees for the first time, and statistics showed that around 16,000 people died across Europe as a result of this heatwave. In 2023 we saw land temperatures in Spain hit above 60 degrees. It has been predicted that this extreme weather will only become more frequent and more extreme as the years go on and the global temperature level continues to rise. On top of this, extreme flooding has been causing havoc throughout England, causing deaths and displacement from homes. There is no doubt that climate change is going to affect the way in which every single individual lives in their homes.

I remember in 2022, I was up in Leeds during the hottest day of the year visiting tenants across the estates. For the first time I was receiving complaints about how hot tenants' homes have become. Residents showed me pictures of temperatures above 50 degrees inside their homes. For many, this meant they were struggling to live, breathe, sleep and exist. The homes in the UK simply weren't built to handle this kind of extreme weather and for many, it's going to take its toll. A lot of social homes that I have been into have windowless bathrooms and toilets, poor insulation, and if they are at the top of a housing block, the heat builds to unbearable levels. These homes feel like ovens. For the worst cases, another campaigner and I organised for fans to be sent to families, to try and help them and their children stay cool during the hot summer. It is not a long-term solution to a problem that is only going to worsen – when do these homes become too hot to live in? What happens then? The UK Climate Change Risk Assessment Evidence Report (2021) explained that 'people are at risk of overheating in their homes. This risk is also already classed as high magnitude as there are an estimated 2,000 heat-related deaths per year, which could more than triple by the 2050s.' When the population spends 90 per cent of each day indoors, and there is good evidence to show that 20 per cent of homes already overheat outside of heatwave events, there is every reason for us to invest in fixing this problem and ensure building regulations are enforcing safety for the homes of the future.[2]

The winter months are in stark contrast and heating demand dominates energy use in housing.[3] Poor quality insulation is a key reason. Added to this the rising cost of heating and causing many tenants to be freezing in their homes. Some get so cold that they can see their breath and others have ice inside their windows. Beyond just being uncomfortably cold, the creation of mould due to condensation is a big health and safety concern. Energy companies seem to feel no remorse in allowing costs to rise even as their profits rise too, and these rising prices are impacting the most vulnerable in our country. I have heard countless stories of families not able to switch their heating on during winter because they can't afford to or having to choose between being cold and being hungry. Beyond this, flooding is a severe risk to UK housing and can cause long-term and severe impacts on well-being as well as damage to properties – of which we have so few already to meet the demand. The Climate Change Risk Assessment report states that 'approximately 1.9 million people across the UK are currently living in areas at significant risk of flooding from either river, coastal or surface water flooding. This number could double as early as the 2050s.' The overall bill for insurance claims for properties affected by floods will be in excess of £3 billion.[4] This is money that could have been invested in preventative measures and hard-line defences in the first place.

As climate change progresses, all of these issues will be expedited. The three regions of London, the East and South-East of England have a housing stock of more than 9 million homes, all designed and built with a different climate in mind. The Three Region Climate Change Group has conducted an immense amount of research into this and describes how important it is for us to act now 'to retrofit and adapt our existing homes to increase their resilience'.[5] Their study shows that not only is this possible and cost-effective but that also the adaptation measures will reduce CO_2 emissions and save water. As I've emphasised previously in this book, change in housing is not some idealised dream, it is a practical and realistic solution to the problems we see in our country. If homes are not built in order to withstand the extreme weather, then we will have a much bigger problem twenty years from now.

The housing crisis as it currently exists is also negatively impacting our environment and harming our planet. For example, trying to rebuild from our major deficit will have an environmental effect due to the use of materials (if they are not eco-friendly, which often the cheapest materials aren't) as well as noise pollution in local areas as housing is built. Furthermore, the lack of repair and safe demolition or restoration of older buildings means that materials such as asbestos continue to be a problem. Asbestos is significantly damaging because when construction, demolition, mining and manufacturing activities release asbestos into the environment, it contaminates the air, water and soil (where it can easily be disturbed and redistributed into the air). It can be carried long distances by wind or water before settling and because asbestos does not break down or biodegrade, it poses a significant risk to humans.[6] Although specialist measures would be taken, especially when it comes to the demolition of buildings in order to contain the asbestos, there's no guarantee of completely ensuring safety. This shouldn't prevent us doing the work to build and refit housing; instead it shows us how important it is to do so, because the quicker and more efficiently we solve this problem, the less environmental impact we'll have in the future.

Climate change is a scary and ominous part of our world today, but it's also something that is salvageable with the right steps and investment. The impact of global warming won't be felt as one singular life-altering moment. Instead, it will be a building of different challenges over years. For example, the UK Met Office reports that 'by 2070, the chance of exceeding 30°C for two days or more increases – a lot. In fact, over the southern UK, it becomes sixteen times more frequent than it is today.'[7] Heavy rainfall will increase by up to 20 per cent and by 2070 the hourly rainfall exceeding 30 mm threshold used by the Met Office will be reached twice as often as it was in 1990. The warnings are clear, frank and sobering, and developers and social housing providers are going to have to prepare in order to guarantee the safety of tenants up and down the country.

Social Housing Regulation Bill

On 20 July 2023, the Secretary of State for Levelling Up, Housing and Communities, Michael Gove, brought forward the Social Housing Regulation Bill which received royal assent and thus was made law. An example of the domino effect inciting change, this bill is positive in a myriad of ways, and its policies include:

- Introducing more proactive consumer regulation by the Regulator of Social Housing, with regular inspections of the largest landlords.
- Allowing stronger enforcement powers for the Regulator to take action when landlords do not meet the standards required.
- Giving the Housing Ombudsman additional powers to publish best practice guidance to landlords following investigations into tenant complaints.
- Allowing powers to set strict time limits for social landlords to address hazards such as damp and mould, as part of Awaab's Law.
- Facilitating powers to set new qualification requirements for social housing managers.

Although this bill is a huge step in the right direction, it's far from an immediate solution, and feels to me to be more of a reactive response to our crisis of housing and overcrowding, than a proactive change. For many of those who are struggling within social housing in the UK, any benefit or impact from the regulation will take years to be seen. As tenant numbers increase, and more are forced into confined spaces together, there is no doubt that problems such as damp and mould will skyrocket. But my biggest concern is how this legislation is going to be monitored and enforced. While it's all well and good having laws written down and bills created, it means nothing if they aren't monitored and enforced. In fact, it's no longer worth the paper that it's written on. The state of social housing in the UK is not an issue that's going to be fixed overnight, therefore it is crucial that there is a structure to enforce this bill that has been brought in to protect people. There is no doubt that there are going to be areas of this law which need to be improved and it's about finding where those areas are as soon as possible. We need to reinforce this bill which has taken years to create and become law.

Only days after the Social Housing Regulation Bill received royal assent, *Inside Housing* shared that spending on existing homes jumped more than 50 per cent for housing provider Platform Housing, as damp and mould focus has created a flurry of activity.[1] Although in the first instance this sounds positive, to me it was a sign of how bad the neglect had been. It signified that the sector was aware that damp and mould was an issue, but as a whole had chosen not to address it. Now that they are being forced to tackle the crisis head-on, it is coming to light just how widespread the issues are, and how common the health and safety concerns have been. A day before this bill came into action, the regulator for social housing proposed that consumer standards would now require social housing landlords to physically inspect all homes. Why was this not already a requirement?

Having spoken to and come in contact with many MPs across Westminster over the last few years, I've heard from them time and time again that housing takes up the majority of their casework. So surely it's better for them that this issue is addressed once and for all? Yet even still, MPs tell me they find when advocating on behalf of renters, especially social housing tenants, that local authorities and housing associations divert blame and accountability from themselves. In light of the death of Awaab Ishak and the extensive report by the Housing Ombudsman in regards to damp and mould, housing providers have been told that they can no longer direct blame on to tenants for this disrepair. They were also told that they could no longer use discriminatory tactics as a weapon without a full investigation. So yes, change is coming and the Social Housing Regulation Bill is a good step in the right direction, although to take just one step at this point is too small an action. We need to take a great long leap to resolve the level of systemic problems we're facing.

The Media's Responsibility

As a child I was an avid viewer of the news. My dad loved the news – it would be on in the morning, during the day and in the evening. It was the background noise in our home. My mum loved *ITV News*, and my favourite presenter growing up was Mary Nightingale. She was always 'the 'face of UK news' to me. I never imagined that one day I would walk into that newsroom and meet her, along with the whole news team. I did laugh afterwards at the fact I knew the names of pretty much every single correspondent who was in that day. That should show just how much my parents watched the news.

Journalists were an enigma to me, and their trade even more so. Where did they live? Where could you find one? Contact one? I'd never even met a journalist until I started on my campaigning journey. And I had no idea how the news was actually gathered. Now my mobile has around fifty phone numbers of journalists, who regularly ring me asking for help. Obviously, I like some more than others and I know the ones who are committed to bringing change in social housing, and the ones who think I'm a quick hit for a 'case study' to fill their programmes.

'Case study' was another term I hadn't heard of until 2021. It means a person, a human being, who is at the centre of a story and who journalists want to use to put on camera and tell that story. And so, I learned, human beings are a commodity in journalism. But those journalists who treat people as just a commodity are the ones that I won't deal with. It's not just me, either. People in distress, at the so-called 'bottom' of the pyramid, are the first people to spot a fake. They aren't fooled by a charming member of the press, oozing sympathy and concern in order to get an exclusive. They know who to talk to and who not to talk to. And so do I.

If you google the word 'journalism', the definition comes up as 'the activity or profession of writing for newspapers, magazines, or news websites or preparing news to be broadcast.'[1] It doesn't mention anywhere that journalists should hold the powerful to account. But, to me, that's an essential tenet of journalism. Journalists should speak up for those whose voices aren't being heard. And fight their corner. But they hadn't. The stories of people suffering in social housing had hardly made the news agenda at all. Why was this? To find the answer, I asked Jonathan Levy, the Executive Editor of Sky News, who kindly agreed to speak to me.

Jonathan, who wasn't quite as cynical as me, explained that the intent is there to hold powers to account, but that the general view is that 'the mainstream media, the traditional media, is in cahoots with people in power'. He went on to tell me: 'I don't think that's true at all. I think that the intention is honourable and it's a good-faith endeavour and we really do set out to hold people to account. If journalism is about one thing, it's about who controls the narrative. And the whole point of journalism is to make sure that nobody powerful controls the narrative.'

He went on to say that mainstream establishment journalism is like an exchange. This means the journalists have 'access to people in power to hear about things, and be the conduit for things that the government and other organisations want to get out into the world', and that this information must be used responsibly. Jonathan says the best way to explain this is with an example, such as the early days of the pandemic. 'Mainstream news organisations were briefed by the government about what was going on and had a responsibility to use that information properly and not scaremonger.' However, in some cases, the media did feel as if it was worsening anxieties. Jonathan thinks that 'the danger of this kind of arrangement is that it may dull mainstream news organisations and prevent them from asking the questions, the acute questions, as much as they should. Did we ask the right number of questions about whether schools should be closed and what the impact would be? Did we ask enough questions about whether it was necessary to insist that everybody was vaccinated and punish people who weren't? Did we ask enough questions about whether it was right to bail out the banks? Because we also felt we had a responsibility to make sure that the financial system didn't collapse.'

In spite of some of these things, Jonathan does believe that 'mainstream and establishment media is a good-faith endeavour'. But he thinks that there is a 'tension that establishment media has as the receivers of a certain amount of privileged information through organised channels, the lobby briefings, and using that information as responsibly as possible.'

I think Jonathan touches on an important issue here in his description of the 'establishment' media. The British establishment is the group that, in essence, controls or dominates British society. And the mainstream national media are, in my opinion (and very likely Jonathan's too), very much a part of the 'establishment'.

For example, in May 2022 the *Press Gazette* reported that some 80 per cent of journalists come from professional and upper-class backgrounds,[2] and Sutton Trust research in 2006 found that over half (54 per cent) of the country's leading news journalists were educated at private schools,[3] (which account for 7 per cent of the school population as a whole). I asked my friend Sarah O'Connell, who was one of the first journalists I met, what she thought about all this and she told me, 'I know my colleagues don't live in social housing. Most news journalists don't live in social housing. They have good jobs in national news and are earning good money, and the likelihood is that they came from money.' If this is the case, then it's no wonder that the stories of people living in squalor on council estates have been missed or under-reported.

As Sarah said, seeing the state of social housing when she visited my estate, sadly, didn't shock her. Instead, she added, 'What shocks me is that journalists didn't know it was happening.' Sarah described to me one house she went to see where there was 'water dripping through the ceiling'. The resident had two small children and was incredibly distressed. Sarah produced a report, alongside correspondent Daniel Hewitt, on the state of this home and it headlined on the ITV *News at Ten*, which surprised and elated her, 'as it's very competitive to get a story on top of the ten and it meant that poor housing was being taken seriously.'

It's stories like this that take real tenacity to push to the forefront, and as Jonathan Levy explains, 'The first time you come along with a story that is off-agenda, it's off-agenda for a reason. Nobody takes it that seriously and the journalist who's pushing it has to be really persistent, dogged and committed and know that it is something really important to get it heard.'

Sarah O'Connell has been one of these persistent journalists, or, as she describes, 'an enduring pain in the ass to my editors'. She went to the Grenfell Tower two days after it was burning, as her boyfriend had lived in the area and was concerned he might have lost friends in the fire. She said it felt incredibly weird and upsetting to spectate on people's graves. But what struck her the most 'was a wall that was covered in writing of people who were missing and those who had died, but interspersed throughout the whole wall was condemnation of the news media. How we'd let people down, how we'd betrayed people, how we'd ignored people.' This was in stark contrast to 'half of the world's media and all UK media, all national news channels, all local papers, television crews, famous presenters and a million journalists surrounding Grenfell at that time. I personally don't blame the people of Ladbroke Grove and the people who lived around Grenfell for feeling resentful. Because we could find the time to film them dead or dying, but we couldn't find the time to speak to them before it happened, could we?'

Sarah goes on to say that she understands the animosity that was directed at national news media by the public standing around Grenfell Tower that day, because 'we often don't represent them. We don't always work in the public interest. We don't know how they live. We don't fight their corner when we should. We don't always cover their stories.' She describes how shocked she was to find that Jon Snow, a respected journalist and then presenter of Channel 4 News, shared that he had not been in a tower block in nearly forty years. She wonders how many journalists are like him, and I wonder that too. There are many journalists, I think, who wouldn't step foot on a council estate. Some out of fear, but also out of the assumption there isn't a 'story' there to be told that is easily accessible to them. This leads to the media being incredibly out of touch and inaccessible to those who really need them. Sarah expresses that, 'if we're not living next door to them because we earn three times what they earn, then it's our duty to seek them out. The onus is on us to find them, not for them to find us, because they don't know how to find us.'

Perhaps this is exactly why Grenfell struck such a chord. It wasn't just any tower block or any estate; it was one in the prosperous borough of Kensington. And it also turned out that the tenants of Grenfell Tower had been lobbying journalists to cover the story[4] before the tower burned down, but had been rebuffed, probably because the journalists had little understanding of what it was like to live in such dire conditions. And how unsafe that can be. For the wealthy of the borough, the homeowners, the housing story was counting how much their homes (and their bank accounts) had increased in value.

In respect of this, Jonathan admits that housing coverage on the news has been skewed in the favour of homeowners, not council tenants, and suggests there's still some way to go, saying, 'I don't think we tell enough stories about housing, or we do tell stories about housing, but we are reporting on the housing market instead of houses.' He also believes that 'it comes back to the whole point about diversity. In newsrooms and in many industries, diversity is a kind of end in itself. It's good to have a diverse workforce because it's nice and representative and everybody can feel comfortable. It's *much* more important in journalism to have a diverse workforce because it's a means to a better journalistic end, and very few people in newsrooms these days will have experience of poor housing or even small housing or council housing.'

For me, it's quite worrying to hear the lack of representation of lower socio-economic groups and social housing tenants in the media, but I'm also heartened to hear that a man in Jonathan's position is aware of it and working to change it.

Sarah's perspective here is slightly less positive, saying, 'Through the years, I don't think very much has changed. I think awareness of social housing has changed, but I think the behaviour of journalists fundamentally hasn't changed much at all.' Surprisingly, Sarah adds, 'I think that some politicians have more understanding of what's going on in the country than journalists do, because politicians have surgeries every week and most of them will make it to that surgery. So I think they're more in tune.' I would agree, because I have also seen this in my investigations and discussions. Maybe it's also because politicians knock on doors to campaign and, in the majority of cases, this will involve knocking on doors in a council estate or two, at the very least.

There is no doubt that there is change that needs to take place within the media, and these insights from Jonathan and Sarah demonstrate to me that our news system is somewhat flawed; one that may have good intentions, but one that also has blind spots and areas of neglect. This is adding to a domino effect on poor housing, meaning it's less likely to be highlighted, discussed and, therefore, resolved. Just like the broken houses I've reported on, the news media is also littered with disrepair and needs fixing – with better representation, more of a connection with the general public and less reliance on powerful institutions for stories. Rectifying this would be a great step forward but, having spoken to them both in depth, I don't think either Jonathan or Sarah would disagree with my conclusions.

So now I hope you can step back and see the bigger picture. The three pillars of our society – housing, education and healthcare – are impacting the wider world around us in a myriad of ways. But ultimately it's the human impact which is the most distressing. Ordinary people, like you and me, forced to live in the harshest of conditions, who see little to no hope and whose lives are cut short. It's hard for anyone who lives in comfort to fully understand the difficulties being faced in our own country, but in illustrating all these ramifications of poor, underfunded housing, my hope is that something will strike a chord with you and you might see the urgency of taking action and rallying those in power to make a change.

The dominoes continue to fall and the fractures in our society are spreading – just like a small crack in glass. If you don't fix it, it will grow and worsen over time. The end cost will also be more, and you'll be kicking yourself thinking, 'Why didn't I do something earlier?!' We will all be doing the same if we let things crumble beyond this point. Here, I've wanted to show how many different parts of society are influenced or impacted by housing, and vice versa. No matter which area of society you are in, mending this issue and averting this crisis now will have a distinctly positive impact on your life, your future and your children's futures. So now, I want to look to that future. I want to take you through the motions of how we can get there and what it might look like if we do take action. I want to leave you with a plan that feels doable and positive, one which you can press into the hands of authority figures across the country, and take the news media with me. And I'm optimistic that I can do that.

Part Four:

Looking to the Future

What if housing was affordable for all? What if public housing was destigmatised and built to represent modern society? It sounds almost utopian, like it couldn't possibly exist. But it can, and it does in places like Vienna and Singapore – two cities that probably aren't going to have to grapple with the cost of living crisis around the world quite like we have to here in the UK. Both cities are case studies of what social housing could be if we made the necessary investments in its future.

The main thing that the housing sector really needs is funding. Everyone knows this, whether they live in temporary housing or a fancy town house. It's something that government after government has refused to properly acknowledge, and that failure is what has brought us to where we are today. It always seems like people in positions of power would have us believe that these issues are simply too big to resolve and too expensive. That there's no other way for things to be. This is not the truth. Not only do other countries do a lot better than we do financially, they also prove that if we properly invest in solving the issue of housing, other social issues like employment, quality of life, health and well-being will improve. Ultimately, having a roof over our heads is a cornerstone to a functioning society. The money is worth investing.

These other countries are living proof that we can solve the issues of our country, and we can go from crisis to prosperity. It may take harder-line rules on the wealthy, and it may require higher taxes for a time, however, it will result in better livelihoods for the many, not the few. These are lessons in longtermism. What is longtermism? Longtermism is the ethical view that positively influencing the long-term future is a key moral priority of our time. It is not about thinking solely about the here and now, but considering how we might resolve issues for the future, even if the fruits of that future feel a long way off. Longtermists believe in prioritising problems such as climate change, housing and rising technologies such as AI. There are complaints that longtermism diverts too much attention away from current problems in the world, and so I believe it's an ethical standpoint that should have more balance. For example, instead of 100 per cent of our government output being used to rectify smaller day-to-day immediate problems, what could happen if 30 to 50 per cent of that output was invested into resolving long-term, entrenched structural problems?

There are plenty more key questions we should be asking to try and work out the best possible way to resolve our crisis, and create a fairer future, and while I don't have all of the answers and will not pretend that I do, I want to offer some ideas to hopefully catapult the conversation forward. As well as us activists and grassroots campaigners on the ground, we need thought leaders, scientists and economists desperately to contribute and offer their insights. This is my design for the future, and I hope experts will engage, argue with and add to this. I hope I will be challenged and I hope that we can all work together to find a real concrete solution.

Singapore, Vienna, Germany and Europe

In Singapore, public housing looks like any other building and 80 per cent of the population of 5.4 million lives in the housing. Social housing isn't a place where people who are struggling end up, it's a place where people from all walks of life live. The irony is that the original public housing policies in Singapore were actually started while it was under British rule. When Singapore became independent in 1959, only 9 per cent of the population lived in public housing, and it was clear that what the British put in place was a failure.[1] So almost immediately after becoming independent, they started over from scratch. In 1960, the Singapore Housing and Development Board (HDB) was formed to provide affordable and high-quality housing for residents of this tiny city-state nation. Admittedly, they did have it a bit easier than we do – things like planning permission, acquiring land and, most importantly, money were not as large a problem and the housing sector got heavy investment. However, they achieved brilliant things and set regulations to prevent home ownership from taking over: the development board prohibits Singaporeans from owning more than two residential units at any time.[2]

Safe housing wasn't the only thing they thought about when they built all of these homes, though. They also invested in transport with their light rail and subway systems, and they built schools, gyms, shops and all the dedicated amenities you would need to live well in the areas where they were building new apartments, meaning residents would have access to everything at their doorstep. There were even communal spaces for weddings and celebrations, and the government subsidised more expensive properties, meaning that rich and poor people live side by side in social housing and there is no stigma at all about living there, with census reports showing residents reporting a 90 per cent satisfaction rate.

I should say that it really wasn't, and isn't, perfect – there was a lot of taking land from owners when it was 'in the public interest', so by 2005 the government owned 90 per cent of Singapore's land. There is also a bias towards married couples with children when it comes to available subsidies, so the system isn't all roses, and there are a lot of big cultural differences that would make it hard to replicate in places like the UK. However, it shows the positives that can come when housing isn't an afterthought. How could we do this sort of thing in Britain? Is it possible? In the case of Singapore, probably not, at least we couldn't replicate it identically – can you imagine our government making a land grab? There is no way anyone would trust that policies like this wouldn't somehow be used for the personal gain of the top 1 per cent of the country. What is aspirational though is that housing is such a priority to the government, and there is clear satisfaction because of this.[3]

A lot of people in the UK would turn their noses up at living in social housing, because of the stigma attached to it. But what if social housing looked like any other apartment building? What if it was well built, had good amenities and was maintained? I think a lot of people from all sorts of different backgrounds would be happy to live somewhere affordable as long as it was clean, safe and warm – I believe that all that negativity we have in the UK would fall away. In fact, during the 1950s and 1960s, this was the case and there was a lot less stigma attached to social housing. The possibilities that come when we invest and remove stigma are real and exciting. The unrelenting pessimism and demotivating feeling that nothing will change, or that this is all too hard a goal to reach is simply the institutions winning. There is always potential for radical change; history has proven that time and time again. It starts with united efforts and loud voices and continues with resilience and persistence. It's about agitating the status quo and questioning it when it doesn't serve the majority. The examples to do things better already exist and we aren't reinventing the wheel, so we're already closer than we think.

Then, there's Vienna.

Social housing policies in Vienna have been shaped by the political commitment that housing is a basic human right. Access to quality, affordable housing has helped vault Vienna to the top of the world's most liveable cities. Although they were built to house the poor, Vienna's Gemeindebauten, or council estates, did not become ghettos: named after figures like Communist Manifesto author Karl Marx or the Italian anti-fascist Giacomo Matteotti, the buildings were designed to be indistinguishable from private buildings housing the city's bourgeoisie. Care was also taken to integrate them into the fabric of the city. – POLITICO.[4]

Vienna's politicians made housing, social housing and affordable housing their priority many decades ago, during a time when many European countries and global nations believed it was the right decision to sell off social housing stock. Vienna instead maintained their commitment to keep as much housing stock as possible, and also to continue building. In the Austrian capital, more than 60 per cent of residents live in 440,000 social homes, around half owned directly by the municipal government and the rest by state-subsidised, not-for-profit co-operatives. It is known that after the First World War, Vienna had some of the worst housing conditions in the whole of Europe. Now they have some of the most sophisticated and successful housing structures and models in the whole world. Through the focus on housing and quality housing, Vienna has been able to build thriving communities where residents have an overall good quality of life. They've been able to integrate families from different backgrounds and classes, from vulnerable lower classes depending on social housing to some middle-class families too, all living among each other. The aim of this was to help prevent a divide between classes and groups in society and also remove the stigma that social housing has had across countries for many decades.

Vienna is a perfect example of how society thrives when they have security, affordability and stability within housing. Many of those living in social housing in Vienna have tenancies which are lifelong, choosing to move only when their home can no longer accommodate them or the size of their families or perhaps when they choose to move on and buy their own home. Vienna's land use strategy has also led to cost efficiency for the city when building social homes. In Vienna, if you have a large plot of homes for multi families, it's a requirement that two thirds of that has to be for social or affordable housing and the other one third can be for market rate. There is also a consciousness for lower rents within social and affordable housing because it's understood that will mean more individuals and families have more disposable income that can be spent and reinvested back into the local economy. Rents are regulated by the city government so that none of the residents pay any more than 20 to 25 per cent of their household income for housing. This is incredible if you look at the comparison with the UK where rent is on average 53.6 per cent of annual income, rising to 80 per cent in London's more expensive boroughs.[5] Vienna has also begun building with climate change in mind. Their aim is to lower their carbon footprint by better insulating homes and introducing passive cooling. They are playing their part in helping to tackle climate change without reducing the quality of life for residents. Taking these proactive measures as opposed to being reactive, they are actually thinking about the quality of life for residents in many years to come and trying to ensure they have the best quality of life possible. Their collaborative housing system means that not only are the new homes being built affordable, made to last, and made to create a community, but residents can also help design their own homes and are consulted through the process. They can decide to add co-working spaces, rooms for seminars, communal kitchens – all sorts. It means these new urban areas are built with a strong community behind them ready to move in. On top of all this, Vienna is also one of the most affordable cities in the world.

Vienna is easier to compare to the UK. Their public housing blocks have been built continually since the 1920s. They started building social housing around the same time we did, but when we stopped building, they continued to meet the demand of their growing population. They also brought in legislation that we have either not considered or have voted down – there are more strict rules protecting renters, meaning they can have security and know they aren't going to be moved on with no notice. This means people in Vienna often stay renting and aren't too worried about needing to buy their homes to ensure their security. Unlike the model in Singapore, which would probably be hard to replicate anywhere else, the model in Vienna would have been totally achievable if we'd just continued to match their steady rate of building.

Maybe parts of that model could still be adopted – for example, their government subsidies to private companies who commit to building social housing that is affordable, of a high quality, and is forward-thinking in terms of use of space and sustainability. Vienna's government will also subsidise renters if a new build ends up being too expensive. Maintenance on their 500,000 affordable flats remains a priority. When areas are gentrified, social housing gets updated to suit the style and modernity of the rest of the area, so there's never the dated, deteriorating council blocks you see in the UK – it all blends in. All of this means that social housing there is much less classist – people from the middle class are just as likely to live there as working-class people. The catch of all this is higher taxes – that subsidy has to come from somewhere. Also, construction costs in other countries are often a lot lower than in the UK and the US. In spite of this, there is still a lot to learn from Vienna, and if our government got a handle on the huge amounts of wasted taxpayer money (as much as £5.6 billion in 2020), something like this might even be within our reach.

Beyond Vienna, there are some countries in Europe that have proven that, when done correctly, the rental sector is able to thrive rather than financially cripple vast swathes of the population. Germany, for example, has more people renting than owning properties. It is believed that people prefer to rent than to own their home. In fact, Germany has the greatest proportion of home renters in Europe – only 39 per cent of the population own the homes that they live in compared with about 60 per cent in Britain. German tenants typically enjoy a lot more freedom when renting, and an example of this is them having control over the interior of the property, painting and redecorating without the need to let the landlord know. This is a feature of one of their 'indefinite' rental contracts. Having said that, if a tenant takes on a newly decorated apartment, they are expected to return it to the same standard when they decide to vacate the property.

Still, on the whole, this is different and more progressive when compared to privately renting in England and the UK, where tenants are expected to inform landlords of any decorative changes to the interior of a property during their tenancy, and are expected to return the property to the original condition when they depart. This, in a lot of cases, makes tenants feel as though they are restricted in their own home and makes them fully aware that in fact it is not their home. However, the biggest and most noticeable difference between the two countries' rental markets is in the security of renting. The system in England of tenancy law is loosely regulated. It is not compulsory for private tenants to enjoy a right to a written tenancy agreement, although most tenants will have one (CAB 2016). Most rental contracts signed after 1997 will be assured shorthold tenancies (or ASTs), which typically provide security of tenure for generally a year or less. These tenancies would be considered short compared to other European countries like Germany. If the landlord and tenant agree, tenancies can extend beyond the defined period in the contract. However, this 'rolling contract' period provides tenants with less security than the initial contract period.

Greater flexibility in rental agreements and varying expectations between landlords and tenants in the UK's rental market leads to relatively brief tenancies. In England and Wales, the average tenancy duration is a mere 2.5 years, a span further shortened in high-pressure housing markets with reduced risks of vacant periods. In contrast, in Germany, most tenancies are established on an open-ended basis. Research employing the German Socio-Economic Panel Study indicates that as of 2010, the typical tenancy period in Germany extends to around eleven years, with the median length being roughly six years since 2006.[6]

German law predominantly supports these indefinite tenancies, allowing exceptions only for certain types of 'tied' accommodations. Within the sector, there exists some diversity. Notably, the upper echelon of the market tends to feature shorter tenancies – about eight years – compared to the lower end, where tenancies often extend to roughly thirteen years. The factors behind this distinction remain unclear from the available data, whether attributed to more mobile tenants in the upper market segment or affluent tenants in that category terminating contracts early due to property acquisitions. Furthermore, the prevalence of longer tenancies in Germany signifies a cultural preference for a more extended investment outlook among landlords.

Germany's real estate market has experienced sluggish house price growth for decades. Coupled with a tax system that encourages prolonged investment by gradually diminishing capital gains tax on properties held over a decade, fewer incentives exist for landlords to sell properties, thereby maintaining continuous tenancies. In line with this, the higher quality of rental properties and guaranteed rent stability may encourage tenants to stay put. This stability benefits both tenants and communities at large. Infrequent moves lead to greater schooling consistency for children and enhanced opportunities to build community connections and engage in local activities. However, a delicate equilibrium is needed. As Kemp and Kofner (2010) aptly state, 'Residential mobility is relatively low in Germany, a phenomenon arising from and contributing to the extended leases and robust tenure.'[7] Tenants in Germany possess the right to challenge tenancy termination if they can demonstrate that it would cause hardship for themselves, their families or households. These rules are designed to strongly prioritise tenant security, providing them with ample time to secure alternative suitable housing and manage changes in employment or other life circumstances. Landlords are given three months in such cases, a longer period than typically seen under English Assured Shorthold Tenancies (ASTs), allowing them more time to find new tenants and reduce the risk of empty properties and loss of income. Landlords can also choose between 'immediate notices' or 'specific notices' to terminate tenancy agreements, both requiring specific reasons. Immediate notices might be triggered by issues like significant rent arrears or criminal activity in the property, resulting in prompt termination. Specific notices apply to legally prescribed situations, such as the death of a tenant when the family does not wish to continue the tenancy. Exceptions to these rules are scenarios where the landlord resides in the same property.

Unlike England, where policymakers have stepped back from rent regulation in the private rented sector (PRS), Germany has taken proactive measures to shield tenants from rent hikes, utilising both first- and now second-generation rent controls.[8] The 'first' generation model typically sets a cap on rents relative to local market rates, while the 'second' generation model limits rent increases during the tenancy period for individual tenants. This second-generation model has played a long-standing role in Germany's rental market, controlling the extent of rent increases within tenancies. Landlords can set the initial rent when the property is listed. This approach is fortified by robust tenancy rights. Over a three-year period, rents cannot surge by more than 20 per cent, and landlords are bound to maintain rents at a certain level for at least twelve months. Tenants have a month to decide whether to accept a rent increase and, if declined, they receive an additional two months' notice before moving out. This structure ensures tenants fifteen months of renting at a fixed rental amount. The effectiveness of second-generation controls is evident, with long-standing tenants paying significantly less rent compared to local market rates. Despite this success, in 2015, the federal government introduced 'the rent brake', allowing state governments in high-pressure housing markets to set a maximum local rent ceiling. This regulation prevents landlords from charging rents exceeding 10 per cent above the local average for similar properties. This rule applies only to new tenancies, and tenants cannot renegotiate retroactively if their current rent surpasses the local ceiling. To prevent adverse effects on the development market, newly built homes are temporarily exempt from rent controls. This legislation has been implemented in Berlin, Hamburg, several major cities in North Rhine-Westphalia, and over a hundred municipalities in Bavaria.

Beyond Singapore, Vienna and Germany, there are countries all over Europe revolutionising social and public housing, building with intention in ways that are eco-friendly and greenlighting projects that will decrease stigma. These housing projects also encourage social mixing. For example, the Global South and East build spaces where mixing communities who represent a range of ages, cultures, backgrounds and finances is a highly important factor, and this can have a positive impact on disadvantaged communities. It can improve employment opportunities, provide access to better quality services and an improved quality of life. A report did find though that social mixing requires a hierarchy of spaces from private to semi-public to public to allow for social interaction, and that sometimes such enforcement can result in a diminished sense of community when those around you are different to you. Japan has been taking real action to promote integration in their housing, in the hope that there may be more support systems for their rapidly ageing population.[9] But again it is Singapore who really stands out: 'As an independent city-state that emerged from racial conflict and a colonial past in the 1960s, Singapore provides a unique case study of successful implementation of social mix housing policy.'[10] They have quotas for each of the main ethnic groups (Chinese, Malay and Indian) applying to each apartment block and 'as a result, Singapore is characterised by very low levels of racial residential segregation.'[11] While other parts of the Singapore policy we may not be able to introduce, an idea such as social integration is one that should definitely be encouraged.

Finland is another country famed for its affordable housing, which supports social mixing and brings down homelessness. Why? The right to housing is 'enshrined in the Finnish constitution'.[12] Around 25 per cent of new homes are social housing, and they want to increase this to 35 per cent. Their policies have also 'been instrumental in preventing segregation and facilitating work-related migration'. This is something clear in London. As the cost to buy and rent rises in certain boroughs, people are forced to leave, and these areas that were once rich with cultural and economic diversity become sterile and made up of a wealthy population. The displacement of poorer inhabitants of these spaces means that some areas have little to no diversity of ethnicities, religions or classes. Communities pool together in areas they can afford, and while London is a multicultural hub, when you move beyond the centre it is abundantly clear where different communities are able to reside. There are huge learnings here for the UK, and there have been multiple academic reports done that give key learnings from social housing of other countries, and explain in detail how these changes were made. The resources we have are abundant, and the answers to our problem are readily available; now we need to act.

Attitudes towards Housing in the UK

The most effective and immediate change that could be made in the UK is the attitude and understanding of what housing means, and what social or council housing really is. Our housing situation can't truly be fixed until we treat it with the respect that it deserves. A home isn't just an object that represents peak capitalistic success, nor should it ever be seen as the American or British dream. It's not an asset that represents and defines an individual's worth, nor is it a luxury that only some of us should have access to. It's time that we – and by 'we' I don't just mean the general public but those that govern us too – viewed housing and having a roof over our heads as a fundamental right and instilled it into consciousness through investment and policy changes.

This crisis has happened because what is a necessity has turned into a surplus comfort that can be bought. It has driven those who already have vast amounts of wealth to add to their wealth and hold this all close. This crisis won't be fixed if the British political understanding doesn't change into considering housing as a worthy and important investment that benefits all areas of society. Perception has power, but perception is also fundamentally biased and often untrue. Many perceive that social housing is a sign of being inferior, simply because those who live there have less. It is deemed a worst-case scenario and those who live there are demonised. Words have power too. Shifts in our language are important to move from perception to reality and I think the key phrases 'social housing' or 'council housing' should change. They hold too much judgement which has been piled on to them over the years. A simple language change to *affordable housing* has a much more positive sound and is the same phrase used in many other countries who have successfully destigmatised their housing projects. Affordable is what everyone wants. It doesn't mean 'paid for by the council' or that the properties will be rubbish; it simply means they are affordable according to people's means.

Still, there is no doubt that antisocial behaviour within social housing is a problem. It is one that reinforces stigma but is something that isn't taken nearly as seriously as it should be. In the past I've had numerous complaints from residents specifically about antisocial behaviour, ranging in severity from people being attacked to extreme noise or disorderly conduct. In a lot of these cases, antisocial behaviour impacts the mental health of the victims and there have been times where some residents were afraid to even leave their homes. I have, on a few occasions, tried to intervene by speaking with chief executives at housing providers that were not taking individual cases of antisocial behaviour seriously. Residents are forced to jump through hoops when making a complaint, but much like when reporting disrepair, it almost seems as though doors are closed in your face when you are most in need. I do believe the next government should make it a requirement for landlords to have to respond to cases of antisocial behaviour within a certain amount of time, and laws and legislation need to be revised to ensure the safety of those in housing. Resolving issues like this, and making sure affordable housing is a safe, supported space, is essential to removing stigma and misunderstanding that all social housing is dangerous or full of those who are a problem. It's not true, because there are people who are antisocial everywhere, but if the protocols are not in place to support and protect, then these issues build.

There have previously been conversations about social housing giving way to affordable housing, to shift attitudes to be more positive. Affordable housing is owned by private companies, as opposed to social housing which is owned by the council. It's true that we could enforce regulations similar to other countries, so that any developers must allow for 30–40 per cent of the housing they build to be affordable. However, the idea of affordable housing has already been introduced here and it hasn't taken the world by storm. It is not enforced or regulated, and the affordability is entirely dependent on market rates and locations. The government states that affordable houses are 'homes let at least 20 per cent below local market rents or let at rates set between market rents and social rents. The market rent or market value refers to the cost of housing either for rent or for sale in the private sector. Calculating market costs takes into account the property size, type and location.' The fact that all of these things can impact the affordability of this affordable housing means that is often not affordable. Ultimately, the costs are being calculated by the private companies developing the homes and there is a commercial pressure to make sure these homes still allow developers to incur a profit. Kunle Barker, property expert and broadcaster, shared the reality of developers building affordable housing, stating that 'the problem is that there is nothing affordable about building homes in the UK. So how are developers supposed to provide affordable homes on their schemes?' To make projects work and for them to be commercially viable, building affordable homes makes no economic sense. And that's the problem. The privatisation of housing, and the lack of public funding and investment, means that it has all become an economic endeavour instead of a social improvement one. Affordable housing should, in theory, be a good thing by replacing some of the urgent need for social housing, and in other countries it is clear that it can be. However, affordable housing can never replace social homes, and it would be a huge mistake for us to go down this route as other countries have done.

Beyond this, the government needs to look after the housing we have, add to it and expand its amenities, as well as bite the bullet on building more. Or they could enforce regulations similar to other countries, that any developers must allow for 30–40 per cent of the housing they build to be affordable housing. By improving our housing stock, we remove any distaste around them not looking attractive or being run-down and in disrepair. If affordable housing could be desirable and attainable, it would ensure that less exploitation could happen. Standards would be met and people would have a higher quality of life. There would be less shame attached to living in subsidised housing or housing supplied by the government, and if there were community spaces around it could be a major way we resolve another crisis, the crisis of loneliness, which can increase the risk of mortality by 26 per cent.[1] Ideas can shift and change, perceptions can adjust, and awareness and positivity can change things. So here's a challenge directly aimed at people who *don't* currently live in social housing. I'd love you to answer these two questions yourself, and reflect on whether you carry a bias. Awareness of it is the first step to changing it for good:

Before reading this book, what did you think of social housing? Be honest with yourself.

Now you've read this book, what do you think? Has your mind been changed?

Resolving our Rents

Now, I have said throughout this book that social housing, private renting and home ownership are all linked. I don't believe they can be fully separated out, and I think affordable housing is the real priority. However, the private rental market is really at breaking point and so we need to consider our options for change here. The market for private rentals feels the most exploitative. Renters are being used as pawns by homeowners so they can pay off their mortgages. Regulations are minimal and rights aren't as set in stone as they are in somewhere like Germany. We have a systemic crisis on our hands, and the way to fix it is undoubtedly going to make a lot of landlords very, very mad. However, without doing so there is literally no end to the price-rising and piss-taking of the rental market. According to Foxtons Estate Agents, property rents have even increased as much as 20 per cent in 2022 alone.[1] If this were the case with food or water there'd be a national outcry, and the government would be forced to respond and step in. But for some reason the needs of renters are not looked at with seriousness.

There is an opportunity for us to change this but the government must listen, not just to understand but to respond. Rents should be reduced and frozen at a certain average percentage of wage income. There should be more regulations in place that restrict the ability of landlords and estate agents to keep raising prices, and these need to be properly enforced. We can take some learnings from Germany where tenancies are longer, with flexibility to decorate (within reason) to make it feel like a long-term home, and within this the tenants should have more rights. Also, if a landlord has multiple properties, perhaps a proportion of those properties should be affordably rented, so that they are actively contributing to change and not just collecting the pay packet. Personally, I believe it's important for the government to drive as many bad and unscrupulous landlords out of the private rented sector as possible by shifting the policy to not just allow them to make financial gain without clear reason and fair and honest housing supply.

Any decent landlord would agree that there is no room in the private rented sector for landlords to be exploiting tenants, allowing them to live in disrepair, or bullying them out of their homes because they choose to raise concerns about an issue. We need to make it clear for private tenants what their duties are as well as making it very, very clear to private landlords what their responsibilities are by providing homes for those who rent. I believe all landlords in the UK should be registered, in a similar way as having a passport or a driver's licence or a National Insurance number, which gives them permission to operate as a private landlord in the UK. This is a way to drive out illegal lettings and will mean the government has the means to check that landlords are meeting the rental standards. Section 21 must go. Using a section 21 notice means a landlord doesn't have to give any reason for asking you to leave, and I don't believe that should be the case for tenancies. It has resulted in families being turfed out on to the street, with no explanation as to why. Any landlord wanting to evict the tenant should have fair reason as to why they want to do so and there should be evidence. Removing someone's shelter, a human necessity, requires more investigation and evidence than a single notice.

The government should also take action against holiday lets and big corporations like Airbnb operating in major cities up and down the country and incentivising private landlords to switch to making their properties holiday lets. This reduces the amount of rental stock available for those who need to keep a long-term roof over their head in the major cities where they work and live. We've also been seeing in coastal areas families being pushed out as a result of holiday lets growing and small coastal towns being ruined as a result. On top of this, and what I would say is the most pressing issue of all when it comes to the private rented sector, is the skyrocketing rental prices. As I've mentioned before, but it bears repeating: average rent far outstrips average wages in the UK, and in London, it is dire. For a long time, there has been lip service around rent controls or regulation of rent being brought in, but no government has actually committed to acting. The current Mayor of London Sadiq Khan is calling for rent regulation, yet even Labour have made no commitment to looking at and regulating rent to make it fair and affordable for renters. If the government were able to do this, it would bring affordability and stability to the private rented sector and as a result it would mean fewer people would be driven out and dependent on social housing, easing off the pressures for local authorities. Imagine if the dominoes could fall in the *right* direction for once.

Improving Housing

Archive footage and films such as *Cathy Come Home* show very different social housing buildings than what we see today. Neglect has led to disrepair building over decades, and leaves us with buildings that are boarded up and taped over. Glass is broken and walls are thick with moss and mould. Original buildings were built well for their time; however, modernisation has always been needed to ensure that they withstand the test of time. Just like in rentals, standards are not being upheld. This level of neglect has led to lives ending, and I am a firm believer that in situations where unlawful deaths have occurred, there should be scope for criminal prosecutions against landlords. Currently, it's not the case, but if we are really going to change the way in which tenants are treated by providers, then I think the idea of criminal prosecutions in worst-case situations would force accountability, responsibility and change.

An area that is often overlooked when it comes to talking about the state of housing here in the UK is temporary accommodation, because, by the end of June 2022, there were nearly 100,000 households in temporary accommodation. This accommodation is, more often than not, overcrowded and in disrepair, a lot like the social housing stock that we have. However, tenants often feel as though they have fewer rights, with there being little willingness to listen from local authorities. They are fearful that if they complain about the conditions they are having to live in, they will be told to leave and be provided with no more assistance by the council. Often the most dilapidated buildings you see are temporary. The 'temporary' part somehow creates even less responsibility to make them liveable, although temporary accommodation is often the opposite of temporary for many. There needs to be a change in the way that we provide temporary accommodation and the quality at which we provide it. Currently, we have a decent homes standard which isn't fit for purpose, and therefore another standard should be created which includes temporary accommodation. We also need more temporary accommodation as well as social housing, because, just like social housing, there is an ever-growing demand for temporary accommodation while residents wait for social housing property. Local authorities are haemorrhaging money to employ companies to do a job badly. There are situations where people have been placed in converted sheds, garages, shipping containers and converted offices as temporary accommodation. The government has even suggested converting disused high street shops and takeaway shops into accommodation. This isn't improvement, it is a reactive plaster over a bigger problem.

Improvements also need to take into account climate change, as discussed at length on pages 169–174. There is the fundamental disrepair, and then there is the additional work that should be invested in to protect people from the ever-shifting environment. At the end of the day, it's money. It is funds that are required to shift the dial. The ideal would be that it comes from big business, where a tax is added to help us towards these goals that will, ultimately, result in greater economic prosperity. Energy companies could be an incredible source of these funds. Instead of putting billions into harvesting resources that are scarce on our planet, they could help towards bringing greater stability and protection from the environment. This feels like a pipe dream, but it's one I'm willing to stand behind.

When it comes to privately owned houses, changes also need to be made quickly. The days of promoting home ownership as the only route to a successful life are gone. Doing so has sent us into an economic crisis for the majority. Home ownership should perhaps be a distant goal and strategy for the government, rather than an immediate one. This would require adjusted messaging to both appeal to those who long to own houses, while easing their concerns about feeling they need to do so as soon as possible for their security. There should be communication that legislation will be brought in, as I've flagged above, to protect tenants who rent for the long term, and then policy that may help first-time buyers to eventually get on the ladder. For example, and this may be considered controversial, parents should only be allowed to contribute a certain percentage of deposit to their children when they want to buy a house. This may be frustrating to some parents who want to give their children more of a leg-up, but it will create greater equality when it comes to first-time buyers in the market. Ultimately, though, I believe home ownership should not be encouraged by our government until there is greater stability in our social housing and rentals.

Home ownership isn't the fairy tale that we were once all promised and it certainly isn't easy because we've seen this in these times of economic crisis where those paying off mortgages can also suffer turbulent times. This notion of home ownership being the be all and end all has diverted attention away from the fact that housing isn't just a financial good or an asset or a way of making extra income. While I understand that politicians know the idea of home ownership is a popular policy on the surface, they should also understand that it is a reality for mostly an older demographic of people in the UK. If they have any hope of bringing around the younger voters, they need to consider alternative means to help them feel supported. That being said, according to the National Housing Federation, 'older people today are particularly vulnerable to poor housing that can cause or worsen health conditions, reduce a person's quality of life, and can even result in premature death. Close to half of England's 4.3 million non-decent homes are lived in by someone over 55 years old.'[1] This shows that when it comes to housing and poor quality housing, it's not only an issue for young people, but it also affects our elderly community too. There is real incentive to change the policy they lead with, and to capture more of the realities of all generations, rather than just the privileged few.

Now, nothing can be improved without regulation. And our regulation needs to be significantly strengthened and increased when it comes to repairs, regulations of landlords and their responsibilities, regulation of rent in the private sector, but most importantly regulation in terms of the quality and safety of social housing and new builds. Grenfell was promised to be the turning point when it came to safety and quality of our homes, but more than seven years since, the prevention promised simply hasn't been rolled out effectively. I've seen developers being paid large sums of money to do the bare minimum, which has included bypassing basic safety standards. Cutting corners is still happening everywhere. Under David Cameron's coalition government, regulation and red tape were slashed, and it was this that resulted in so many tragedies within housing. Homes should be built to last, with quality in mind. They should be practical and also consider the lives and the lifestyles of those who will eventually be living in these properties, for example those with accessibility needs. By doing this, it will give the government a chance to catch up with the demand up and down the UK. The goal should be to eradicate poor-quality housing in the UK. The government should ensure that developers are scrutinised routinely to make sure they're building to a high standard and that corners aren't being cut in order to make a profit, or to save money at the expense of public health and safety. The disaster that was Grenfell should not just be a lesson but a defining moment in history that is never repeated.

Economic Benefits

I'm under no illusion that all of the above is a tall task, given the people that are in charge of the country and making decisions. I understand that some people might read this and laugh at my idealism, my hopes for change. But I won't be caught up in the negative and entrenched view that shifts can't happen, and I'm young enough to keep pushing and to hopefully see them come to fruition. I've seen enough of the horrors and suffering that can happen if we continue with inaction and I want to see the benefits and progress that can occur if some of my suggestions become reality. And these benefits, while they may not be immediate, will be significant and long-lasting. I think some people underestimate the power of having shelter or a roof over your head, or perhaps they don't appreciate it as they should. The positive impact it can have on the quality of your life is unbelievable, but you wouldn't necessarily know that unless you had experienced the alternative. I remember when my family and I were in terrible, broken and unsanitary accommodation, and that overwhelming feeling it wasn't a safe home, a place to rest or recuperate. Instead, you are in limbo, you are uncomfortable consistently and you are full of shame. You question if this is what the rest of your life is going to be like, and you wonder if you can sustain and continue with that existence. You have no refuge and no hope. So, of course, the alternative to this is deep contentment, where the safety and security of your surroundings is mirrored in how you feel. It is somewhere to restore yourself after a long day, where you can clean yourself and make yourself a meal, and it allows you space in your mind where before it was full to overflowing with worry. The benefits in this personal sense simply can't be overstated.

I want you to imagine now that you woke up this morning, and your bathroom ceiling was caving in because of a leak upstairs; or you found cockroaches crawling around your bedroom. Imagine if you woke up to black mould all across your kitchen walls; or you had sewage overflowing in your toilet. Further still, imagine you had no home at all and you were living on the streets, with no protection from the elements, only cardboard and the cold air to welcome you to sleep. Some of you don't need to imagine; this may be your reality. But for those of you who do need to, I hope this has made you feel uncomfortable. Because most of us, even I, can hardly deal with no hot water for a few days, so it helps to picture yourself in these positions, putting yourself in others' shoes, to recognise how problematic it is that our housing is in such turmoil. By appreciating this, you can appreciate the joys of the alternative. Where you can have the headspace to live and thrive, instead of just survive, because that's what so many in the UK are doing today and every day – surviving. It is about worth and dignity. We should all have the dignity to have a safe, warm home to go home to. We are all worthy enough for this to be a right.

ECONOMIC BENEFITS

The individual benefits are hard to quantify in any way other than anecdotally, which makes them less of a benefit to strive for. So, to speak the language of the government, I want to argue that the benefits will result in economic productivity and prosperity. The economic benefits of fixing the housing crisis would be fairly mixed in the short term, with large investments and not-so-immediate reward. However, in the long term, the benefits would be great. Lack of access to housing for those that are homeless or in temporary housing makes it incredibly hard for them to maintain a stable job, and the mental toll on those who live in poor accommodation makes it hard for them to function or be as productive as they might want to be. By resolving housing problems, many more would be enabled to work and contribute more to our economy. This, in turn, would contribute to our wider society. If the 1.4 million people waiting to access social housing were supplied the homes they need, they would be able to commit more to work and achieve their goals of studying or a career. Because they would have more income, they would rely less on social welfare and benefits. They would spend more, lifting the economy. Similarly, if rental prices were to be controlled, it would allow those living in private accommodation to save and it would increase their disposable income, encouraging consumer spending that would pump money back into the British economy.

Lifting the ban on allowing asylum seekers to work here in the UK would, it's believed, contribute £1.6 billion to UK GDP every year. Although controversial politically, migration makes sense economically. Even with migrants travelling from countries affected by war and other forms of persecution, there are many migrants travelling to the UK who have qualifications and experiences in various professions which would be beneficial and add to our skilled labour force. Even with migrants who don't have high-level qualifications, there's room for them to fill essential jobs that as a country we need the labour force for. There are definitely ways in which the government could use migration in order to benefit the people of this country, instead of weaponising it as a scapegoat to the detriment of our economy. It was said early in 2023 that a decrease in immigration to the UK since Brexit has negatively impacted the UK's labour supply. It is said to have led to a shortage of 330,000 workers in Britain. Yet, at the end of 2022 there was a backlog of more than 166,000 asylum claims here in the UK. Although asylum seekers coming to the UK can't work, many wish to do so and I have worked with asylum seekers who say they'd love to work and provide for themselves, as opposed to living on around £35 per week in poor accommodation. As well as the economic benefits to allowing asylum seekers to work in the UK, the right to work would also provide social benefits for them. It would provide them with a better standard of living, setting them up to stand on their own two feet and provide for themselves, and it would allow them to engage and integrate better into British society at a faster rate.

Allowing asylum seekers to work would save the government and taxpayers £6.7 billion per year, as well as increasing tax revenue by £1.3 billion from those migrants. It's believed that the UK has the most restrictive policies out of all European countries. In the EU member states, asylum seekers are allowed to work nine months after waiting for their applications to be processed. In Canada, asylum seekers are allowed to work immediately and in the US they are allowed to work after six months of waiting for an application to be processed. No doubt these countries feel the economic benefits of allowing these people to work. Compare this to the UK where, in some cases, we are paying for asylum seekers' livelihoods for more than ten years while they wait for their application to be processed, instead of allowing them to work and provide for themselves. Ministers do suggest that allowing migrants to work in the UK would attract more migrants to take the dangerous risk of crossing the Channel. However, if there were safe means and security attached to our increased acceptance of migrants, then we may have an opportunity to remedy some of our economic crisis. In the first quarter of 2023, the UK's GDP shrank by 0.3 per cent, but there is an opportunity here to help the economy grow while also giving dignity back to those fleeing war, persecution and poverty.

Building new homes has clear economic benefits. According to our own government's report, building new housing supports the economy by providing employment. They state that 'In 2021, one in twenty jobs in England were in the construction sector – approximately 1.3 million jobs.'[1] New residents in these homes increase spending in the local areas, and it creates social networks for people. More affordable housing improves housing stability and allows those housed to make more contributions to the economy.

As mentioned before, dilapidated housing results in poor health, and when people have poor health they contribute less to the economy.[2] Austria has seen that investing in new, affordable homes has positively impacted their economy, with their Limited Profit Housing Associations 'estimated to add an additional 600 million to 1 billion Euros to Austria's GDP every year'. Their residents have more purchasing power and spend more, and 'the public purse saves money (e.g. due to lower expenditure on housing allowances, higher tax income from other consumer goods) and is able to spend more on other areas, which in turn leads to higher GDP.'[3] In the UK, the housebuilding industry already 'supports 600,000 jobs, contributes £19.2 billion a year to the UK economy, spends £5.5 billion with suppliers, 90 per cent of which stays in the UK, pays £576 million towards community facilities including £225 million towards education facilities alone and generates a £3.8 billion spend in local shops and services'.[4] With all of these positives, why shouldn't we invest more into this industry?

One of the biggest barriers to decent housing here in the UK is the cuts in funding to local authorities over the last decade or more. Instead of investing in local councils and housing departments, we have resources stretched beyond capacity. The reality is you cannot fix the housing crisis without investing in local authorities. Not only does the government already expect local authorities and housing associations to build the homes that we need for the future, but it also expects them to provide a high service and maintain their current housing stock. There is only so much that you can do with limited resources and local authorities have been doing as much as they possibly can over the last decade or so. Disrepair in social housing costs local authorities vast sums of money when they fail to deal with it. According to *Inside Housing* magazine, of the seventy councils to respond to the freedom of information request on cases, sixty-five (93 per cent) local authorities had seen an increase in 2020–21 when compared with 2017–18. Of those authorities that provided figures for every year, the total costs increased by 77 per cent from £7.9 million in 2017–18 to £13.8 million in 2021–22.[5] Local authorities are going to need billions in order to provide the service needed by the British public. Investment in them is the only solution to push us towards a better housing reality, otherwise they will have no incentive to do the right thing by people. The money would need to go to existing housing stock, improving their conditions and ensuring they are safe. Beyond this, if the new renters' reform bill comes out, it would put responsibility on local councils to regulate the behaviour of landlords in the UK, and if they lack resources already, such regulation would undoubtedly fall through the cracks. Investing this money might feel to politicians like an unnecessary spend, but if they continue to cut public spending instead of investing, the crisis will only become further embedded and the disrepair, and resulting deaths, will continue to happen.

I believe there should also be separation between social housing providers and developers of social homes. What we've seen over the last few years is that social housing providers have lost their purpose and instead are focused on becoming property developers and knocking up homes as quickly as possible in order to meet government targets and receive government funding at the expense of their existing housing stock and their tenants. Social housing providers should solely focus on providing a good service to their tenants, while social housing developers should be a separate entity tasked with building social homes up and down the country. These homes will eventually be passed over to social housing providers for them to distribute to those that are on the social housing waiting list. I believe this will enable a refocus of the social housing sector and it will also make it clear what the responsibility of each entity is. Though harder to enforce, I think this could have a significant impact on our social housing.

The long-term economic benefits that would amass if the right adjustments are made should be incredibly attractive to our government, especially in today's economic climate. Access to good housing enhances the overall quality of life for citizens, which in turn positively impacts their engagement in both the labour force and overall productivity. The long-term economic growth would be substantial and undeniable. Countries with good housing options are more likely to attract and retain a skilled labour force of people from across the globe. Secure housing provides individuals with a sense of belonging and this can lead to better mental health, reduced stress and improve overall focus on work responsibilities. Better living conditions reduces exposure to health risks and diseases and this therefore leads to a healthier workforce, resulting in fewer sick days and increased labour-force participation. Stable housing can improve access to quality education and children in stable homes are more likely to attend school regularly and perform better academically, setting them up for higher skilled jobs in the future, which maximises their overall contribution to the British economy. Need I say more?

Social Benefits

Society has taken a lot of beatings in the last few years. We've had the pandemic, the cost of living crisis and with ongoing wars across the world, it can feel like we are still on unstable ground. Community is harder than ever to access, despite us having greater means to do so through our digital technology. Once again, I want to bring your mind to the hierarchy of needs. As a society, we are not tending to our most important and essential needs. The physiological and safety needs of housing, warmth, security and safety are in flux for so many in our country, and therefore we don't have the strong foundations to create spaces of belonging and love, and we don't have the money to pour into our communities and our loved ones. If we can work towards resolving this crisis, the benefits to our society will be great. There will be more space for the communities and relationships we desperately need, and there is no greater reward in my eyes.

The most vulnerable in our society are the ones most without the stability required to form stable relationships and communities. By fixing the housing crisis using a bottom-up approach, we could see the reversal of the current ever-increasing rates of homelessness in the UK. Currently, we are seeing record levels of homelessness, largely driven by the cost of living crisis and a lack of social housing. We are also, tragically, seeing an increasing amount of child homelessness in the UK too, with 139,000 homeless children in England alone (an increase of 8,000 in three months), with record levels in temporary accommodation. If the government builds more homes and temporary accommodation, we could provide homes to many vulnerable homeless people. If they make rent more affordable, some homeless people may even be able to rent privately. Resolving the housing crisis, of course, isn't the only solution to homelessness, as in many cases multifaceted support is required for individuals to sustain a stable life. However, by tackling one area we will make progress. Once again, other countries are living proof that you can have low levels of homelessness. Iceland, for example, has the lowest homeless population on the European continent, with 349 people homeless per night. Why? Because in 2018 the government made tackling homelessness a priority and they made goals to build homes for homeless people. Japan is the country with the world's lowest rate of homelessness. This decline is a result of initiatives undertaken by local authorities and regional NPOs and involves diverse strategies of giving those who lack housing access to resources, permanent shelter and community assistance.[1]

When it comes to child homelessness, I really feel there is no bigger shame, and these children and young people deserve stability in their lives. If we resolve this for them, our younger people would develop better, and they wouldn't have to carry the shame and stigma that might follow them later on in life. I've spoken to young people growing up in poor conditions and they never want to invite their friends around, and I know that feeling because I didn't, either. They just don't want the judgement that might come along with it, even if it's imagined. Providing these kids and young people with a home will allow them to just be themselves and not have to shoulder worries that are bigger than them. They will have more headspace to commit to their education. When I worked in a school it was interesting to see the close correlation between those who were showing signs of behavioural challenges and those who were homeless. Early education is crucial for a child's development and future prospects. If they struggle there then they will likely be at a disadvantage in their future education and careers. We have to remember that these young people are our future generation of workers: there are future doctors and nurses, politicians, teachers, bus and train drivers, social workers; there are the next generation of university students and so much more. We must look after them to ensure they can thrive in society, and hopefully, make it better for everyone. Nelson Mandela once said, 'There is no keener revelation about a society's soul than the way in which it treats its children.' What I'd also like to see is better safeguarding and support for the children, with a shift that would see housing as a key safeguarding issue in the health and education sectors. The government should also give education professionals more powers when it comes to contacting housing providers regarding concerns about our young people. There are doctors and head teachers who already do this, but they are simply ignored. I firmly believe that if an education or health professional has the interests of their young people at heart, and if they are concerned that the health and safety of that young person is being compromised, there should be clear steps to escalate the issue and protect that child.

I remember at the age of twelve or thirteen when my dad, my sisters and I were made homeless and we were having to travel on a daily basis to different hostels in between school. We wouldn't know where we'd be going after school, or whether it would be the same place we'd stayed the night before. I remember it being winter and absolutely freezing. That is a distinctive memory. I remember we would walk and walk and walk till it was dark outside and our socks would be soaked from the snow and rain. Our feet would be cold and wrinkled when we found a hostel to stay in. For these memories to still be with me so viscerally is a testament to how damaging child homelessness is, and during this time I was going to school. If one of those teachers had noticed and had the power to change things for me and my family, maybe I wouldn't have to carry the weight of these memories. Looking back now, I really do feel sorry for my dad because he was trying to do everything he could to make sure that we as kids wouldn't have to be out on the streets. As a parent, I can't imagine what it would have been like in that position with three kids, not being listened to and having no idea where to turn for help. Too many families share this story, or have worse stories, and surely there is no bigger social benefit than eradicating this suffering for as many young people, children and parents as possible in the UK.

If our housing crisis is fixed, it would do wonders to improve the physical and mental health of people across the UK. I was heartbroken to see that, in December 2023, an asylum seeker had died by a suspected suicide, with many people citing the treatment of migrants and the lack of housing or help as the likely reason. Across the UK, we have a suicide rate of 10.7 deaths per 100,000 people.[2] This is appalling, and beyond this, the mental health issues in our population is rising, with many not accessing treatment.[3] Now I'm not saying that improving housing will automatically resolve mental health disorders, since sometimes mental illness is genetic and sometimes it is triggered by entirely separate traumas and realities. However, there is a clear link between poor housing and mental health problems, and research by the NHS confederations stated that 'people with mental health conditions are one and a half times more likely to live in rented housing, with greater uncertainty about how long they can remain in their current home. They are twice as likely to be unhappy with their housing, and four times as likely to say that it makes their health worse.'[4] A happier and more mentally stable population can only mean a better society. Similarly, the positives would be displayed in physical health too, as many health issues can be related to poor living conditions such as hypothermia, respiratory illnesses, headaches, tuberculosis and meningitis.[5] We could ease some of the intense pressure on the NHS by tackling the cause of health issues at the root, and they could have more time and capacity when they aren't required to attend to quite so many patients. The overall benefits of improved well-being across our society are difficult to quantify, but given the link between poor housing and so many negatives when it comes to health, improved housing would surely show exciting new positives in a myriad of ways.

Tackling housing should be a primary mission of the next government. I have said this multiple times in this book, and I believe it and am willing to convince everyone to believe it too. Both political parties state one of their key missions is to drive higher economic growth by tackling social issues, but so far there have been limited examples of such missions completed. Resolving social issues and building a stronger economy will inevitably attract investment from domestic and foreign sources. Wouldn't it be something for us to lead on the global stage in a way we haven't for many decades? While other countries put their investment in the right places, and see the rewards, we are falling behind the curve. The social benefits will reap so many rewards on the widest scale for our country and I want that for us more than anything. I believe we can have it, and I'm excited and energised by the people already leading the way to it.

The People Shifting the Dial

We all have our roles to play in pursuing a better future and getting ourselves out of this crisis, and while in the majority of this book I've been addressing the government and the powers that be to enact the change we need, I also know that change can come from empowering the public and giving voice to the grassroots campaigners. We all have the power to vote, and we should use those votes wisely, analysing what each political party is promising us and considering deeply if this best serves us in the long term. It can be easy to zoom in on short-term benefits, but these promises are shallow and usually don't hold much truth – we don't have to look much further than the Brexit campaign to see that – so it's better to look at what could have benefits way into the future. The saying goes 'short-term pain for long-term gain', but so often I feel that many of us don't subscribe to that thinking. It can feel hard, and often it requires a degree of selflessness, but hopefully I've given enough evidence here that shows a positive result of doing so. Analysis of policy should also go hand-in-hand with analysis of the people who are meant to serve us. We need to hold politicians and officials to account and apply pressure to make sure we see the change we desire. Antonio from Grenfell United expressed this well. He said that if government officials don't achieve the key goals they set out to while they're in their seat in government, they should be removed from their posts. If you don't achieve your goals in the workplace, you have to take responsibility for that and explain why. This should become more of a reality for those in government because theirs are goals that impact us all.

As well as voting and exercising your democratic right, any support given to charities, whether through donating or campaigning, does do something to support families in need, just like the people I have met and whom I describe in this book. To give to needs outside of our own is one of the greatest gifts we have to give, and we shouldn't squander opportunities to be kind, to listen and to be respectful. It isn't just where we invest our money, it's about how we treat each other. Similarly, activism doesn't just have to be the kind of full-time work I do; you can have activism in a number of different ways, such as amplifying voices pushing for change on social media, buying books from these campaigners who seek justice (you've done that already!) and reading widely to gain fuller knowledge on how we can better tackle injustice and unfairness in society. As victims of wider powers, pushing against them can feel impossible and exhausting. I truly understand that, but if we don't then we are sleepwalking into a crisis we may never come out of.

Striking is also one of the only forms of bargaining power people have to be heard and listened to. It's frustrating for some when trains and public services don't work as they should as a result, but it goes to show just how much we rely on the working-class people in our society. These people aren't asking for red carpets, or to be showered with money, homes and so on – they're asking to be able to survive while doing their jobs and to be able to live and work in comfortable conditions. It doesn't sound like much to ask, does it? When people are frustrated with key workers taking action, they are failing to step back and take a look at the real issue here. In every situation, the government has the opportunity to get a better understanding of the issue and negotiate, but instead they dig their heels in. I think it's to somewhat assert their dominance and control. What we're seeing then is that more and more workers feel disrespected and get to breaking point, and they feel striking is their only way to prove that what they do is so necessary. It's a massive lesson, not just to the government but also to people across the country.

There are those who have long known the lessons outlined in this book. There are campaigners across the world drawing attention to all of the issues I've been outlining. I am not the only voice and I'm not the most expert voice but I know my voice is important. I know my voice is all the more powerful when added to the cacophony of voices from today and times past who are drawing attention to social issues, injustices and crises happening around the UK. One incredible campaigner whom I've had the pleasure to talk to is Tom Murtha. Tom Murtha is now retired, but in his time he has done incredible work to improve housing, and social housing, in the UK holding positions as chair, executive leader and non-executive board member and trustee at a number of different housing and social care organisations. Even since retiring, he has campaigned tirelessly for government investment in social housing, and for his work he has been awarded an Honorary Doctorate by the University of Birmingham for his leadership in the housing sector and received a lifetime achievement award for his work in housing and diversity. Tom believes we need to see a return of the social purpose and value that was there when housing associations were set up, as we have moved so far away from these values.

Tom tells me, 'I was born in a council house, raised in a council house and when I was about thirteen or fourteen, my family and I were homeless. It was council housing that rescued us after nine months of what would now be called sofa surfing.' He shared my sentiment that these experiences never leave you, and the value and appreciation he has for things that many people take for granted have remained with him for his whole life. 'It's a basic right to live in a warm, safe, decent home at a price you can afford. That's what I believe. And I believe that we as a country should be striving to make that happen for everyone.' He started his career in 1976 and he really thought that we would have achieved such a thing by now. 'There's been a housing crisis since the day I started my career.' So why are we still not doing anything about it? Is it because the issue isn't 'sexy' enough? Or do too many people simply not care? Tom explains that there was a time where it seemed people did care, and things were progressing: 'At one time, with government investment, we were building 300,000 homes a year and the majority of those homes were council homes. The type of home my family lived in, the type that working-class people, wherever they come from, could afford to live in and afford to rent. It felt as though we'd overcome some of the issues that we wanted to overcome.' So the possibility of progress is there, but it's a shame this didn't continue as we likely wouldn't be in such a dire position as we are today.

Tom has also always advocated for those who are Black, Asian or of other ethnicities within his work. From a young age, he realised the intersection of poor housing and racism, especially when it came to migrants. 'There was a very famous landlord called Rackman who was exploiting immigrants,' he shared, and explained that 'different generations of people coming from the West Indies, Asia, Africa and the Caribbean have had to experience the same suffering immigrants experience today.' And with new racist policies being brought in, I can't see that changing anytime soon. Throughout his time, Tom has sensed 'a real movement away from the original social purpose of social housing. It has become more commercial, more involved in private finance. The lack of funding is still at the heart of the issues we have.' He also said to me that there is specifically a lack of genuine funding that expects little in return: 'There's always a gap between the market rent and the social rent you want to change,' he explained. 'The real investment stopped about the late 1980s.'

Tom has not always received a warm reception when sharing the issues he has seen in the housing sector; in fact he describes being vilified, heavily criticised and ostracised because people felt he was talking rubbish, and that the sector shouldn't have to commit to the social good. Tom shared with me, 'It gives me no pleasure to say twelve years later, that I can say I told you so. Almost everything I said twelve years ago has come to pass.' I'm thankful Tom is out there, still pushing the message and campaigning for better housing. He is fair and realistic in his takes, explaining that he didn't run a perfect business. 'I made some big mistakes in my life; we all do. But I hope I always listened to criticism when it was justified.' Fascinatingly, he was the reason his dad didn't buy the council home he grew up in. 'I told him, that house provided a home when we were homeless. If you buy it, it can't do that again. And I'm pleased to say that the same house in Leicester is still rented by Leicester City Council to a family.' Tom lives by his words, and his actions are nothing short of incredible given the pushback he has had. If more people in power could follow his lead, we could turn things around for good.

Tom Murtha is one voice I felt was important to high-light, but there are others who are out there pushing and advocating to end this crisis. People like Daniel Hewitt who kindly wrote the foreword for this book, Sarah O'Connell, the journalist who is telling our stories, Vicky Spratt, the author of *Tenants*, charity and campaign groups such as Grenfell United, Shelter, Crisis and Social Housing Action Campaign who all work tirelessly to improve the futures of people around the UK. These are people who should be applauded, and I hope in some small way you might, after reading this book, help, support or amplify. There are so many fighting the good fight, and it is them whom I have faith in to help turn this crisis around.

A Letter to My Dad

It doesn't feel right for me to end this book with a conclusion, as there is no conclusion or neat tying up to the issues I've referred to. This is a living, breathing crisis, one which will no doubt have updates and changes and new shocking realities by the time this book launches into the world. I would love to see this book be a part of or even prompt the shift that sees positive change occur, but I am under no illusion that these issues are greater than me and so deeply entrenched that it feels like it needs a miracle, or another tragedy. If Grenfell wasn't enough to set these wheels in motion, I'm not sure anything else will. I still remain hopeful, and I remain willing to use all my powers to end the inequality in the UK, because more than anything I believe in our country and its potential to be somewhere great, and I believe in humanity's inherent goodness and our ability to do better, even in the hardest of times.

Instead of a conclusion, I want to leave you with this letter that I wish I could share with my dad. By including this in the book I want to memorialise and remember a man who was one of the best of us. Who deserved so much better than the treatment he faced. He, just like so many others we have lost in the years of crisis, of neglect, of austerity

233

and wealth inequality, should have a legacy, and this book will be the start of ensuring they live on.

While they weren't able to see a country out of crisis, maybe we can.

If tears could build a stairway, and memories a lane, I'd walk right up to Heaven and bring you home again.

Dear Dad,

This has been the part of this book I've been avoiding, but I knew it was coming. It's crazy to think it has been four years since you passed away. It sounds a cliché to say 'it feels like yesterday', but it genuinely does. Nothing in life prepares you for what it feels like to have a parent pass away; there is nothing comparable to it emotionally, physically or mentally. From the moment you came and saw me getting my hair done and I could tell something was up, that you wanted to say something but didn't know how to tell us about the cancer, to the months watching your health deteriorate but still having hope that a miracle would happen, I have never felt so helpless. Nothing ever prepares a child to see that happen to a parent, someone they expected to be there forever and always.

I often look back on pictures and videos of us because I'm worried that I might forget how you looked or sounded, but even four years on, I have dreams where your voice is clearer than ever. The saddest part is when these dreams feel so much like reality, and in them you defy the odds and beat your cancer. . . and then I wake up, for a split second believing it was real before tumbling back down to earth again. It's cruel. Then again, I also have dreams where you are exactly the same as how I remember you. Ones

234

where you know exactly what to do to annoy me and I tell you to go away. I laugh so much at that now, Dad.

I'll be honest, some days are good, some bad – really bad. There are now more good days than bad, but I don't think the bad days will ever completely go away. I've learned more about you since your passing than when you were here. I've seen a whole side of the family that I never knew, including Grandma. Meeting Grandma in Ghana, I immediately understood where you got so much of your personality. I saw so much of you in her. I learned where you went to school, where you grew up and played football, I met your family friends back in Ghana and learned about the school that you went to, as well as the times you would get in trouble at school. You had an impact on so many people, and I loved hearing all of their memories of you.

Growing up, I always heard about people diagnosed with cancer and passing away, but I could never have imagined this happening to someone close to me. Perhaps I was naïve or ignorant, but I never thought it would touch anyone in the family, until it was you, and you became the one in two people who are diagnosed. Nobody outside of our family will know what that year was like with you, going through all the treatment. The trips to hospital, the blisters in your mouth, when the doctors asked us if we wanted you to be resuscitated after your heart had stopped, but you continued to fight until the end. . .

One thing I'll never forget you saying is that when you're alive you hear from nobody, until they hear of your death. It's then that people you don't even realise you knew come out to say one last goodbye. You were right. I could tell that's one of the things that worried you most about dying, leaving us and the thought of you not being remembered by anyone. . . but you have been remembered, in a way you could have never imagined.

The one thing I don't think I'll ever be able to forgive myself for was the conditions you were unwell in. The place you called home. It's why I go so hard in trying to help so many others now in similar and sometimes identical situations. You fought for years so that we could have a place called home, from being homeless in storage units to living in a garage. You made the best of it, but you deserved to enjoy somewhere you could call home before becoming sick. If I had known then what I know now, perhaps things would've been different, perhaps I could've done something; I don't know what exactly, but something. This is something I'll have to live with.

I am grateful that through your story grew change. Through your suffering shone light. Through your death rose strength and power. Not just in our family but for millions of people in similar situations across the country. Your story is what ignited a flame that's burned strong ever since you left, and I know it has been what has carried me to the point I find myself at today. I know you'd be laughing your head off seeing me on BBC News, *or in Parliament having to speak with politicians, but above all, I know you'd be proud. Proud that you've continued to live on through your kids and proud of the subject I'm speaking about in the rooms that I enter. Access to housing was hell for you and I know it's the one thing you'd want changed in this country for others.*

I spoke to Uncle when I visited him in Washington, and during a drive at night he turned to me and said, 'Imagine if your dad hadn't become sick in the home he was in; imagine things didn't play out like they have and his death hadn't motivated you in the way it has to do the work that you have done.' The people I've helped wouldn't have been helped, the politicians wouldn't have been held accountable and this book probably wouldn't have happened. He's right, and as hard as it has been and while not a day goes by without me thinking of you. . . I know deep down you'd say the same and would be satisfied with how your story has helped so many others.

It's still so hard to sit down and concentrate on writing everything I've wanted to say to you and to the world in this book. It's not perfect, but nothing truly is. I really do hope that one day in this journey called life and death that I will see you again, but until then, the work continues.

You thought we'd forget about you, but little did you know you'd make history. Continue to look down on us, continue to be proud and, most of all, continue to keep that flame burning bright. . . until we meet again.

Rest in the everlasting power and peace that you deserve.

Your son,

Kwajo

Acknowledgements

This book wouldn't have happened without the help of so many, and I am grateful to the following for their work and contribution to this book.

Thanks to my agents at YMU for advocating for me: Meghan Peterson, Francesca Ianelli and Anna Dixon.

Thank you to my editor Katie Packer for everything.

Thanks to the whole team at Trapeze but especially Francesca Pearce, Sian Baldwin and Tom Noble.

All my gratitude to those who offered their opinions, stories and insight for this book including Aisha Amin, Faisal Abdullah, Fasial Farooq, Grenfell United, Edward Daffarn, Antonio Roncolato, Tom Murtha, Moussokoa Palazzo, Anjali and Codie Mcbride. You are all incredible people on the frontline of this crisis, and I hope I have done your experiences justice here.

Christian Weaver, Kelly Darlington, Alice Wood, Daniel Hewitt, Sarah O'Connell, Jonathan Levy, thank you for sharing your expert opinions with me and helping me to refine my understanding of this crisis.

Further Reading

Books

Skint Estate by Cash Carraway
Chavs by Owen Jones
Tenants by Vicky Spratt
Show Me the Bodies by Peter Apps
Down and Out by Daniel Lavelle
Poverty Safari by Darren McGarvey
Municipal Dreams by John Boughton
Generation Rent by Chloe Timperley

Online resources

https://www.oecd.org/social/social-housing-policy-brief-2020.pdf

https://www.theguardian.com/money/2023/apr/28/average-monthly-rents-hit-2500-in-london-and-1190-for-rest-of-uk

https://www.standard.co.uk/homesandproperty/renting/revealed-the-explosion-of-the-ps1-000-room-as-swathes-of-london-become-unaffordable-to-renters-b1072776.html

https://www.theweek.co.uk/business/personal-finance/959309/what-will-happen-to-the-uk-rental-market-in-2023

https://assets.publishing.service.gov.uk/government/uploads/system/uploads/attachment_data/file/759590/Social_Housing_Sales_2017-18.pdf

Endnotes

How We Got Here

1 https://www.kingsfund.org.uk/audio-video/key-facts-figures-nhs
2 https://www.bma.org.uk/advice-and-support/nhs-deliv-ery-and-workforce/pressures/an-nhs-under-pressure
3 https://theicg.co.uk/5-key-concerns-for-uk-schools-in-the-22-23-academic-year/

A Very Short History of the Welfare State, Social Housing and the Right to Buy

1 https://www.housing.org.uk/about-housing-associations/about-social-housing/
2 https://www.theguardian.com/politics/2001/mar/14/past.education
3 https://www.theguardian.com/society/2015/aug/26/right-to-buy-margaret-thatcher-david-cameron-housing-crisis
4 Ibid.
5 https://assets.publishing.service.gov.uk/media/5bfd60b4e5274a0fd-5f9fa10/Social_Housing_Sales_2017-18.pdf
6 https://www.theguardian.com/housing-network/2015/oct/07/david-cameron-kill-off-social-housing-affordable-homes
7 https://www.theguardian.com/commentisfree/2022/jun/09/right-to-buy-homes-landlords-rentals-housing
8 https://www.vam.ac.uk/articles/robin-hood-gardens

9 https://www.theguardian.com/housing-network/2016/jan/13/
brutalist-housing-estates-private-barbican-social-london

10 https://cih.org/news/uk-housing-review-2022-shows-england-s-
right-to-buy-is-a-strategic-failure-and-will-exacerbate-inequalities-
if-left-unchecked

Social Stigma

1 Average household income, UK: financial year ending 2022, Office
for National Statistics, 25 January 2023.

2 Household total wealth in Great Britain: April 2018 to March
2020, 7 January 2022.

3 Analysis by Ben Tippet and Rafael Wildauer, University of Greenwich.

4 https://www.theguardian.com/politics/2013/apr/06/welfare-britain-
facts-myths

5 Ibid.

6 https://uk.news.yahoo.com/suella-braverman-claims-benefits-
street-152817819.html

Party Politics

1 https://www.theguardian.com/environment/2023/sep/21/fact-
checking-rishi-sunak-claims-on-the-net-zero-transition

Mismanagement and Deregulation

1 https://www.standard.co.uk/homesandproperty/renting/london-
rents-income-rent-a-home-boroughs-b1069539.html

2 https://www.ft.com/content/4a533f2a-0303-417c-a868-593ddcd-
f76cf

3 https://landlordknowledge.co.uk/uk-rent-surge-average-room-
prices-soar-10-nationwide-london-postcodes-exceed-700/

4 https://www.bbc.co.uk/news/business-65422183

ENDNOTES

First-Time Buyers

1 https://www.leedsbuildingsociety.co.uk/_resources/pdfs/press-pdfs/press-releases/homeownership-remains-the-crowning-glory-for-millions-of-people.pdf
2 Ibid.

Chronic Underfunding

1 https://www.theguardian.com/housing-network/2017/apr/24/housing-associations-crisis-commercialisation
2 https://www.mentalhealth.org.uk/explore-mental-health/statistics/people-physical-health-conditions-statistics
3 https://www.theguardian.com/society/2022/oct/10/nhs-mental-health-patients-wait-times
4 https://www.mind.org.uk/news-campaigns/news/mental-health-crisis-care-services-under-resourced-understaffed-and-over-stretched/
5 https://www.kingsfund.org.uk/publications/rise-and-decline-nhs-in-england-2000-20
6 https://www.theguardian.com/society/2023/mar/26/nhs-england-staff-shortages-could-exceed-570000-by-2036-study-finds
7 https://www.theguardian.com/society/2023/jan/12/ae-patients-in-england-waiting-over-12-hours-top-50000-for-first-time
8 https://www.standard.co.uk/comment/teaching-crisis-worse-covid-strikes-disruption-pupils-b1057121.html

The Cost of Living Crisis

1 https://www.crisis.org.uk/ending-homelessness/the-cost-of-living-crisis/
2 https://www.economicsobservatory.com/how-might-the-cost-of-living-crisis-affect-long-term-poverty
3 Ibid.

4   https://news.sky.com/story/bank-of-england-base-rate-expected-to-reach-5-5-in-february-already-raising-mortgages-rates-12889758
5   https://www.theguardian.com/society/2023/jun/01/one-guy-uses-us-like-a-larder-the-british-shoplifting-crisis-as-seen-from-the-tills
6   https://www.express.co.uk/news/uk/1768768/stealing-supermarket-self-checkouts-survey

Neglect, Disrepair and True Stories of Lives in Crisis

1   *Women, Culture, & Politics*, Angela Davis (Knopf Doubleday, 1990).

We Need to Talk About Grenfell

1   https://www.vice.com/en/article/k7ag8n/everything-weve-learned-so-far-from-the-grenfell-tower-inquiry
2   https://www.theguardian.com/uk-news/2022/jun/13/britain-should-be-ashamed-of-grenfell-response-says-survivor
3   https://www.theguardian.com/uk-news/2019/jun/09/hidden-mental-health-legacy-grenfell-disaster

Case Study Two: 'If I speak up, they might take my kids away

1   https://www.ncb.org.uk/resources/all-resources/filter/wellbeing-mental-health/housing-and-health-young-children
2   https://assets.ctfassets.net/6sxvmndnpn0s/4LTXp3mya7IigRm-NG8x9KK/6922b5a4c6ea756ea94da71ebdc001a5/Chance_of_a_Lifetime.pdf
3   https://www.theguardian.com/housing-network/2015/nov/11/children-poor-housing-temporary-accommodation-health-education
4   https://assets.ctfassets.net/6sxvmndnpn0s/4LTXp3mya7IigRm-NG8x9KK/6922b5a4c6ea756ea94da71ebdc001a5/Chance_of_a_Lifetime.pdf
5   https://www.bbc.co.uk/news/uk-england-london-67126160

6   https://www.theguardian.com/housing-network/2015/nov/11/children-poor-housing-temporary-accommodation-health-education
7   https://cpag.org.uk/news/official-child-poverty-statistics-350000-more-children-poverty-and-numbers-will-rise

Case Study Three: Survival of the fittest

1   https://www.liverpoolecho.co.uk/news/liverpool-news/weighing-six-stone-barely-able-15762870
2   https://www.theguardian.com/commentisfree/2019/apr/22/stephen-smith-benefits-system-dying
3   https://www.theguardian.com/society/2015/aug/27/thousands-died-after-fit-for-work-assessment-dwp-figures
4   https://www.bbc.co.uk/news/uk-england-nottinghamshire-65577541
5   https://www.theguardian.com/commentisfree/2017/may/04/benefits-assessments-damaging-lives-hardworking-britain
6   https://citizen-network.org/news/government-disability-policy-increases-suicide-rate

Case Study Four: 'There was nothing the family could do'

1   https://www.theguardian.com/society/2023/mar/15/census-black-britons-social-housing-ons
2   https://www.theguardian.com/commentisfree/2022/nov/23/awaab-ishak-death-social-housing-mould-family
3   https://www.judiciary.uk/wp-content/uploads/2022/11/Awaab-Ishak-Prevention-of-future-deaths-report-2022-0365_Published.pdf
4   https://www.hw.ac.uk/news/articles/2022/black-people-are-over-three-times-more.htm
5   https://www.mirror.co.uk/news/uk-news/awaab-ishak-landlord-saw-refugees-29573727
6   https://www.gov.uk/government/news/government-to-deliver-awaabs-law

The Domino Effect

1 https://www.un.org/en/about-us/universal-declaration-of-human-rights

Reinforcing Britain's Three Pillars

1 https://www.mind.org.uk/information-support/guides-to-support-and-services/housing/housing-and-mental-health/
2 https://www.housing.org.uk/news-and-blogs/news/poor-housing-causing-health-problems-for-nearly-a-third-of-brits-during-lock-down/
3 https://assets.ctfassets.net/6sxvmndnpn0s/4LTXp3mya7IigRm-NG8x9KK/6922b5a4c6ea756ea94da71ebdc001a5/Chance_of_a_Lifetime.pdf

A Vicious Cycle

1 https://www.insidehousing.co.uk/news/more-than-14000-social-rented-homes-lost-last-year-as-sales-and-demolitions-dwarf-new-supply-80005
2 https://yougov.co.uk/economy/articles/42453-how-many-people-parents-help-first-home-deposit

Stealing Our Homes?

1 https://www.theguardian.com/commentisfree/2024/jan/28/british-homes-for-british-workers-empty-century-old-xenophobic-slogan
2 https://www.kcl.ac.uk/suella-bravermans-talk-of-a-refugee-invasion-is-a-dangerous-political-gambit-gone-wrong
3 https://www.unhcr.org/uk/asylum-uk
4 https://www.refugee-action.org.uk/about/facts-about-refugees/
5 Research conducted by *Good Morning Britain* and given to me by producers.

6 https://www.theguardian.com/society/2024/jan/25/reform-uk-leader-accuses-tories-of-stealing-social-housing-policy
7 https://www.health.org.uk/news-and-comment/news/existing-evidence-shows-that-immigration-makes-a-positive-contribution-to-the-uk-health-service
8 https://www.thestar.com/entertainment/books/zadie-smith-on-fighting-the-algorithm-if-you-are-under-30-and-you-are-able/article_c7648eb3-a3f8-5d3c-bf57-147f82a3a14c.html

Crime and Domestic Violence

1 Office for National Statistics (ONS), released 19 October 2023, ONS website, statistical bulletin, Crime in England and Wales, year ending June 2023.
2 https://www.bbc.co.uk/news/business-66049150
3 https://www.womensaid.org.uk/information-support/what-is-domestic-abuse/women-leave

What Happens When We Have a Lack of Homes?

1 https://www.crisis.org.uk/about-us/media-centre/rough-sleeping-in-london-rises-by-21-crisis-responds/
2 https://england.shelter.org.uk/media/press_release/274000_people_in_england_are_homeless_with_thousands_more_likely_to_lose_their_homes
3 https://twitter.com/RobertJenrick/status/1254504256423542786

Social Stigma Continued

1 https://www.parliament.uk/about/living-heritage/transformingsociety/livinglearning/coll-9-health1/coll-9-health/

Climate Change and the Environment

1 https://www.ukcip.org.uk/wp-content/PDFs/3Regions_Retrofitting.pdf
2 https://www.ukclimaterisk.org/wp-content/uploads/2021/06/CCRA3-Briefing-Housing.pdf
3 Ibid.
4 https://www.ukcip.org.uk/wp-content/PDFs/3Regions_Retrofitting.pdf
5 Ibid.
6 https://www.in.gov/idem/asbestos/health-risks-and-environmental-impacts/
7 https://www.metoffice.gov.uk/weather/climate-change/climate-change-in-the-uk

Social Housing Regulation Bill

1 https://www.insidehousing.co.uk/news/spending-on-existing-homes-jumps-more-than-50-at-platform-as-damp-and-mould-focus-creates-flurry-of-activity-82453

The Media's Responsibility

1 https://www.britannica.com/topic/journalism
2 https://pressgazette.co.uk/media-audience-and-business-data/journalists-class-backgrounds/
3 https://www.suttontrust.com/our-research/educational-backgrounds-leading-journalists/
4 https://grenfellactiongroup.wordpress.com/about/

Singapore, Vienna, Germany and Europe

1 https://www.economist.com/asia/2017/07/06/why-80-of-singaporeans-live-in-government-built-flats

ENDNOTES

2 https://theconversation.com/a-century-of-public-housing-lessons-from-singapore-where-housing-is-a-social-not-financial-asset-121141

3 Ibid.

4 https://www.politico.eu/article/vienna-social-housing-architecture-austria-stigma/

5 https://uk.sports.yahoo.com/news/london-rents-share-income-takes-124509510.html

6 https://pure.aston.ac.uk/ws/files/24391422/lessons_from_germany_jan17.pdf

7 Ibid.

8 https://www.ippr.org/publications/lessons-from-germany-tenant-power-in-the-rental-market

9 https://www.tandfonline.com/doi/full/10.1080/07352166.2021.1983442

10 Iris Levin, Anna Maria Santiago & Kathy Arthurson (2022) 'Creating mixed communities through housing policies: Global perspectives', Journal of Urban Affairs, 44:3, 291-304.

11 Ibid.

12 https://www.munifin.fi/whats-new/finnish-system-for-affordable-social-housing-supports-social-mixing-and-brings-down-homelessness/

Attitudes towards Housing in the UK

1 https://www.campaigntoendloneliness.org/facts-and-statistics/

Resolving our Rents

1 https://www.standard.co.uk/business/business-news/london-rent-prices-surge-by-20-but-house-sales-losing-steam-foxtons-says-b1065366.html

Improving Housing

1 https://www.housing.org.uk/resources/why-we-need-a-long-term-plan-for-housing/

Economic Benefits

1 https://assets.publishing.service.gov.uk/media/65324c17e839fd001486724b/Fact_sheet_8._Economic_social_environmental_benefits.pdf
2 https://commonbond.org/economic-benefits-of-affordable-housing/
3 https://www.housingeurope.eu/blog-1539/new-study-the-economic-benefits-of-affordable-housing
4 https://www.hbf.co.uk/news/massive-hidden-social-and-economic-benefits-of-home-building-revealed/
5 https://www.insidehousing.co.uk/news/councils-spend-45m-on-legal-disrepair-claims-in-four-years-74295

Social Benefits

1 https://www.developmentaid.org/news-stream/post/157797/homelessness-statistics-in-the-world
2 Office for National Statistics (ONS), released 19 December 2023, ONS website, statistical bulletin, Suicides in England and Wales: 2022 registrations.
3 https://championhealth.co.uk/insights/mental-health-statistics/
4 https://www.mentalhealth.org.uk/explore-mental-health/a-z-topics/housing-and-mental-health
5 https://kineara.co.uk/how-housing-effects-our-health/

Credits

Trapeze would like to thank everyone at Orion who worked on the publication of *Our Country in Crisis*.

Agent
Anna Dixon
Meghan Peterson
Francesca Iannelli

Editor
Katie Packer

Copy-editor
Ian Greensill

Proofreader
Vimbai Shire

Editorial Management
Sarah Fortune
Serena Arthur
Jane Hughes
Charlie Panayiotou

Lucy Bilton
Claire Boyle

Audio
Paul Stark
Louise Richardson
Georgina Cutler

Contracts
Dan Herron
Ellie Bowker
Oliver Chacón

Design
Nick Shah
Jessica Hart
Joanna Ridley
Helen Ewing

Photo Shoots & Image Research
Natalie Dawkins

Finance
Nick Gibson
Jasdip Nandra
Sue Baker
Tom Costello

Inventory
Jo Jacobs
Dan Stevens

Production
Paul Hussey
Katie Horrocks

Marketing
Tom Noble

Publicity
Sian Baldwin

Sales
Catherine Worsley
Victoria Laws
Esther Waters
Tolu Ayo-Ajala
Group Sales teams across
Digital, Field, International
and Non-Trade

Operations
Group Sales Operations
team

Rights
Rebecca Folland
Tara Hiatt
Ben Fowler
Alice Cottrell
Ruth Blakemore
Marie Henckel